Forms of resistance.

Poetry, prose and prose-fiction.

Nigel Pearce

chipmunkapublishing
the mental health publisher

Published by
Chipmunkapublishing
United Kingdom

http://www.chipmunkapublishing.com

Copyright © **Nigel Pearce 2020**

ISBN   978-1-78382-5233

Author biography.

Nigel was born in 1959 and was encouraged to live in a capsule of books. Here he has remained after various unsuccessful excursions into the world. He gained a Master of Arts in English with Merit last year. He also has two B.A. (Hons) Degrees including one in Creative Writing, both at 2/1, He should begin the M.A in Creative Writing next October 2020, all studied with the Open University.
Nigel was first hospitalised at the age of 14 for two years shortly after being taken into the 'Care' of the Local Authority. Like many of his generation he was subjected, at various psychiatric hospitals, to repeated electric shocks, electro-convulsive therapy. On one occasion a doctor merely said: 'What is the weather like today Nigel.' 'It is overcast', I replied. His answer was: 'No, it is Summer, E.C.T. for you.' Also, large amounts of medication which was, on occasion, administered intramuscularly and quite roughly.
The grandiose delusion was that the psychiatric staff as a collectivity cared. Some did and they were like stars in a dark night. Doctors, nurses and cleaners who shared a similar vision or were natural-born carers. However, for the majority it was about a regular income, social life and the power. He once asked a male psychiatric nurse of long-standing: 'Do you enjoy having power over people.' His honest reply was: 'Yes I do.'

This will be his thirteenth book with Chipmunkapublishing whom he would recommend to other writers.

Nigel Pearce

Introduction.

These poems, pieces of non-fiction and prose-fiction illustrate a desire to interrogate both the heart and consciousness of the author but also investigate the products of his imagination and the characters of his fellow humans. For, as John Berryman said: 'The heart is strange' and so, indeed is the mind, this author would add. Particularly for those who wear a mask on the stage of human existence, and who hurl abuse and much worse at those who are committed to creating a better world. Because as Lenin said: 'we must be tribunes of the oppressed.'

Poems.

1. W. H. Auden visited us patients as a Christmas Treat.
2. On hearing of the death of a hippy. (Revisited).
3. Summer Haiku. #3.
4. Haiku for C'.
5. Summer Haiku.
6. Summer Haiku #2.
7. ON M.A.D. [Mutually Assured Destruction] (Revisited).
8. Two tribes, two poetics (Revisited).
9. Lament after a downtown incident observed.
10. In Memoriam a pest.
11. Unrhymed Italian Sonnet.
12. The Bluebottle.
13. The unuttered words.
14. For Ian.
15. Homage to Dylan Thomas.
16. Padraig Anraí Mac Pieria's.
17. An Elegy for Eleanor Marx.
18. Ward 19.
19. Hannah.
20. Winter Voice Haiku.
21. The Asylum.
22. Illusion, allusion and delusion.
23. Adam and Eve.
24. Bleach Bath.
25. The Gym Mat.
26. A previous prose-poem.
27. A second portrait of my dead mother.

28. Lines for Sappho.
29. Two traditional haiku.

Non-fiction.

30. 'New Woman' and Hobgoblins: The Communist Manifesto in 19th-Century Britain and its literary aftermaths. A Study of Helen Macfarlane and Eleanor Marx.
31. The Economic Malaise: - a Marxist analysis.
32. The life and ideas of Emma Goldman.
33. Alice Walker *The Color Purple*: a reading.
34. On Byron *Childe Harold's Pilgrimage Canto IV* and John Keats' *'Ode to a Grecian Urn'*.
35. Turgenev: *Fathers and Sons*. Notes on Realism in literature.
36. Franz Kafka: a Marxist reading.
37. Ibsen: *The Dolls House.*

Prose- Fiction.

38. The Cave.
39. Ward 20, a boy amongst men and Paraldehyde.
40. Easter and Beyond...
41. Petra, daughter of the revolution and her life after release from Stammheim Prison (A tale about the S.P.K).

Poems

W. H. Auden visited us patients as a Christmas Treat,

The applause of literate nurses and pampered patients was deafening, The great poet tending to the needy for a fee, he was not quite Christlike,
I wonder how much these people know about this celebrity poet. I rise:
Spain c:1936 is wiped clean from your repertoire, is it because of ….
Who, is that inmate, snaps Auden, like a military Staff Sargent to infantry, 'Well that is one of our more challenging patients replies the Staff Nurse.'
 Why did you censor 'the young poets exploding with necessary murder.'
  And 'Yesterday, the song at sunset/ The adoration of the Madman/ But   today the struggle.' I will not be heckled by a lunatic, that deluded nutter.'

  A young doctor joins the melee: 'Mr. Auden you did write those lines although
 I understand since your conversion they smart a little.'
'You are all deranged   Doctors and patients keep your fantasies to yourself." A first edition is textual
  Proof.' 'You cretinous idiots, take that.' A non-metaphorical pitcher of water is   Hurled across the hall. It hits the senior consultant who is soaked, dripping wet.
  A chime of cheers cascades from first the patients, a gaggle of giggles from the   Student Nurses and then 'you seem a little overwrought from the Professor, a Pill would put that right, get away from me, I am leaving.' "Not so rapidly W.H.
  You seem agitated, could I venture in need of a little rest, Maybe Ward No.6.

  How very Chekhovian of you Herr Professor, how foolish of you Mr. Auden.

In hearing of the death of a hippy. (Revised).

That herd were thronging to and through,
While I rolled along the old academic slot,
Not unaware of a lime green undercurrent,
The radar is still fine-tuned, clean thirty odd
Years, street woman flies on crystal crutches,
She stops dead 'Arthur is dead morphine OD',
Those buttresses of ice melt and we embrace,
'I am going to see him in the chapel I am now',
She is skimming heaven on crystal meth how Long has she
got; I shake for they are blessed.

He was gentle shadow of a man always said,
The same lines about some Nirvana, I-Ching.
Each death is etched on my heart that bleeds, It is made of
ice but heaves as if molten lava.

Summer Haiku. #3
The summer storms
Rage until rain had nourished
Only barren land.

Haiku for C'
Sun beam sparkled gems
In her hair, the Summer burnt
Rivers until dry.

Summer Haiku.
Until summer rain
Fell, my tears had nourished
Only fallow land.

Summer Haiku. #2.
Until summer rain
Wept only to nourish
This wilted flower.

ON M.A.D. (Revisited
(Mutually Assured Destruction[1]).

The dead have not yet dug themselves from graves,
The resurrection of wormed corpses had just failed,
And yet struck by a shaft of moonlight I still awaited,
Snow lay inches deep, a cloak of innocence clotted
Her blood which had drip, dripped from a blue heart.

It could be a sin to be confused when the Bomb fell,
Without doubt we had clarity our cloud of unknowing,
MAD, we had mutually assured destruction icicle cut,
Gaia ached in her birth pangs in these death agonies,
I awaited her child amongst the moulded tombstones.

That freeze hardened as cold bit, but the Bomb fell,
The coppers came and crammed me in a plain van,
Blurt 'where are you are taking me', the hospital for
Mad, bad and dangerous revolutionaries was reply.
'I see' said the doctor, he turned deep red not dead.

Because just like the patient he was red of marrow.

---

[1] Mutually Assured Destruction was a term used during the Cold War to describe the consequences of an exchange of intercontinental nuclear weapons between the U.S.A & U.S.S.R.

Two tribes, two poetics. (Revisited).

A wide margin on balance sheets is a joy?
On their blue lips it is just seething greed,
They need trophies because they are lost,
That bejewelled pen you posture with runs
Dry, there is no ink oozing from a blunt nib.

The nib used by the masses is forged steel,
It has a sound of thunderous bolts clapping,
It writes on papyrus, parchment and paper,
The internet is flexible like a willow in wind,
We have pens, scribes, sleepers, workers.

The masses are leopards poised to leap,
The prey better begin to click pray-beads.

<u>Lament after a downtown incident observed.</u>

Those with iron hearts walked straight,
By a young girl in peril but there would
Be no lion heart and no chivalric poem,
A lady of withered flowers almost dead,
They did not note the bum deal attempt,
She pleaded 'tip me one mate' 'no way',
Yet hid a tear in pillows of crystal salts.

This dumb poet had his heart torn apart,
He knew the girl thirty clean years ago,
Illusions we never had but heroin habit
We did

In Memoriam.

The call beginning a week of flame from a purgatory,
Until a red button has been pushed a rare rant over,
A handset now sits safely in a plastic cradle answer
Machine, already it has reputed their frenzied story.

An imp had spoken yet again to his Master jealousy,
I am the green-eyed monster but am well medicated,
To an extent not attained so it cannot be fabricated,
The wolf who howls but never learnt to have mercy.

My eye is drawn to the wooden knots in this desk,
A Third Eye sees his gnarled face contorted, sane,
The phone did not sleep, neither did a priest's pain,
I grab the phone, rock a cradle: 'you are just a pest.'

A head begins to whirl, and I see the pest emerge,
I swipe at this unwanted guest with its myriad eye,
Recovering I grab a swot, wallop until it does not fly
From a phone on a cradle on a desk await a surge.

Unrhymed Italian Sonnet.

They had an iron heart walking straight,
By a young girl in peril for her the street,
There was no lion heart chivalric poem,
A lady of withered flowers almost dead,
They did not note the bum deal attempt,
She pleaded 'tip me one mate', 'no way',
Was his hissed reply she was about 16?
A silent scream hid in a sea of salt snow.

This dumb poet had his heart ripped out,
I knew that girl thirty odd clean years ago,
Illusions we never had as 'smack' we did,
Dreamscapes have a shimmering logic,
Entombed in a womb with no umbilical
Cord, it was cut by the dealer's grimace.

The Bluebottle.

The bluebottle is buzzing so bloody loudly,
Boris, darling Boris you have saved us all,
It dipped too low than desired for workers,
Go away hey ho just buzz off away us or...

We spray the true-blue fly with insecticide,
No lift red swot and thwack twat take that,
The dustbin of History opens to the rest of
The Swarm.

Crawl flies, beetles, lemmings to your doom,
For ours is the dawn, the morning and noon.

The unuttered words.

In a country graveyard there are many quenched words,
The words of love and hatred and of forgotten pleasures,
The laments of the hollow dead and their demented wail.
And yes, words of love which remained spoken, silenced.

A family torn asunder by malicious powers, forces so dark,
It had wallowed in the unhallowed ceremonies of midnight,
But play with fire and you get burnt, but so do the innocents,
A saccharine smile fooled so many, yourself but not a priest.

This is an incantation to be named, exorcism for the
demons:

"Vade retro satana"

For Ian.

For Ian I still can weep hot tears,
He was a fresher at Cambridge,
His one mistake was an acid tab,
But did not soar to heaven then,
Or descend into a fierce fiery pit,
No his huge brain was scrambled.

They brought him in to a hospital,
Wild wide eyes but blessed calm,
Would you sit with him, yes I said,
For weeks I was shown how he had
Solved the enigma of the universe,
The playing cards randomly placed.

Ian, began to reconstitute his mind,
Singing his Dylan and Cohen songs,
A guitar strummed if slightly off key,
We loved it not noting the repertoire,
Sad songs sung his smile beguiled,
Discharge was twelve months early.

Frequently he housed me orphaned,
Being ejaculated by dad a damn red,
We were two roamers of the labyrinth,
Our wings melted yet contorted sadly.

One dark dawn slapped us, he hung,

<u>Homage to Dylan Thomas</u>

Yet death did have some domain,
Poets die young and some older,
Dylan your words went to heaven,
Yet I was for in love with a poetry,
Not of stages or the world of fame,
We would not be mourned by dust,
For that random thud of our blood,
You an immortal in poetic etching.

The turn to booze with hazy gaze,
 Morphine blued your gold mouth,
 But dear Dylan these poems are
Not resplendent with a Welsh wit,
Yet trickle from tributaries of you,
With notions of your craft and art.

Padraig Anraí Mac Piarais. 1879-1916.

I rest without the dust of ages,
The grieves of my land lighter,
Now that the people listened,
And rebelled in the ballot box.

Anoint a bride and her groom,
The land and her vaulted sky,
To walk to an alter so awaited,
My ring is placed upon a land.

Nigel Pearce

An Elegy for Eleanor Marx.
1855 -1898

Tussy you are me and were the incarnation,
The heights and depths of seething workers,
A fatal flaw lay deep, a martyred immolation,
To live, to die, to fly and not be like a banker.

A Polish, Jewish, Irishwoman girl of the fight,
Organised the women and girls match strike,
Will Thorn who you taught to read and write,
Comrade of William Morris who did not fight.

You translated Ibsen for benighted masses,
And Madame Bovary with the dead Aveling,
He was death in life a cobra waiting for gas,
So strike he did a vampire sucked your sting.

That prussic acid and chloroform made dead,
Your blood has stained our flag a deeper red.

Ward 19.

Just about fourteen and Fate had cracked,
The bell which had chimed a blunt o'clock,
Discord in my head for Ward 19 had a bed,
And a comrade detained in Care was sent.

A crazed creature keeps hurtling at the walls,
His body had bounced off bruised and bleeds,
Again, again, this was not any game I realise,
These were men, why was I a child confined?

I want to go back to the adolescent unit plead,
Say that again and you have another Largactil…
The last one I swear had almost killed me it did,
No refuge on 19's so in a T.V behind the mesh.

8.35 p.m. The Mulberry Bush goes up the staff
just stare, but bedlam undulates like an ocean,
Replaced by skeleton staff, church firebombed,
A burr of nurses, doctors maintain these scales.

I was back on the Unit when most staff surfaced,
There was a smell of fear, an atmosphere I noted,
Learnt their names Liam, Bernadette, Gerry smile.

<u>Hannah.</u>

Hannah you do not and cannot stop wailing,
It has been weeks and still the tears flow in
torrents, I am so sorry would sacrifice myself,
In your synagogue to wash your stains away.

An orthodox Jewess, a jewel with mousy hair,
Something had snapped in Tel Aviv at age 19,
You went sky high and slept all the way to UK,
I shall not forgive the men, nymphomania mad.

Nobody could console Hannah to raw to touch,
She slid away unknown from Ward 10, so sad,
But is sown with golden thread in my notebook.

Winter Voice Haiku.

His course cold voice booms

Freezes like blizzards, Trotsky

Knew before the blow.

The Asylum.

A house on the high hill had wandered lawns,
Summer kissed lawns but it burnt the patients,
The long stayers had old clothes that did not fit,
Most staff just sat nodding into another's eyes.

The white coated doctor's whooshed around
Like Dervishes until exhausted sunk whisky,
They were Father Confessors in purgatory,
You had better give up hope once in here.

No one had anticipated the demolition job,
It is a housing estate, many are homeless.

Illusion, allusion and delusion.

Crimson crystal reflecting burning embers,
Is this an illusion or an academic allusion
To Dante? sorry no we are in the inferno,
It may not exist for you but is reality to us.

This hell is where we weep and are burnt,
The fire is almost beyond our endurance,

Here the horses gallop snorting red flame,
Your delusion maybe O.D. to find if it real.

Adam & Eve.

She is the breeze that carries a Spring scent,
She is a hurricane wrenching trees laid bare,
Her hand just strokes the poetic lyre with fire,
My lips wandered across her humming body.

Yet we can mourn the day flocked in Eden,
We engendered a species far to destructive,
Now that Paradise lies in tangled steel ruins,
Only the freedom of a funeral pyre can free.

Bleach Bath.

This bath was a variation on a theme,
The big black boot and a clenched fist,
Revolutionaries expect this, even kids,
But their repertoire in a house of Care,

Welcome was written numerically '666',
On that superintendent 's forehead, SS,
An intensive hour, you could cut the air,
The rodent came he locked me in a bath

Room. 'You're are a good boy undress',
He had emptied liquid into a bleach bath,
About four inches slightly diluted, 'get in',
'All communists are dirty', he just drawls.

Never met him again he was brought in
To teach me a lesson and soften me up,
                    He failed.

<u>The Gym Mat.</u>

S.S, the superintendent did not like politicos,
At least not red rebels in his Care institution,
We were several boys and girls, the minority,
His tricks are well known to his kind, to divide.

In an assessment centre one summer evening,
He sunk beneath the line of decency as were
Expecting, child-care officers arrange the bout,
A gym mate boxing gloves two of us we refuse.

They whip the other children into the hysterical
Mob, we stand alone resolute for half an hour,
Comrade said: 'I will have to hit you', we dance,
Sparring and then a blow is landed, blood is red.

A previous prose-poem.

He sits in a luxurious sea of crimson cushions observing a solitary lightbulb. It is suspended, like his mind, by a single cord. This is pulsating slightly, or so it seems; no, it is the bulb flickering. The room, it is like being in a cube of pure white, is caressed by fingers of light and shadow. The darkness is merging into the dawn, which is peeping through green curtains, they are hung on steel wires suspended between two hooks, the Alpha and the Omega. He finds his feet and glides around the bulb to discover a yellowing square of plastic, here is the switch, he clicks it off, the bulb is extinguished and so is his mind, it's cast into an ocean of crawling patterns that dissolves into mirrors of soft wax. He locates the switch again, pushes the button on and the knowledge of electricity envelopes his awareness, but the dawn lurks outside, there is the world. In that place lurk purple serpents with eyes composed of composite deceptions, ice which burns like the Sulphur of hell, flee knowing I am both ice and in this purgatory perhaps That torn and twisted red heart you see before is not cold or black, it beats too much.

A second portrait of my dead mother.

 You were confined in sorrow,
Quietly entrapped by a drama,
An ivy script slowly bound you,
The actress performed without
An audience, weeping the mask,
Had dissolved on a stage of dust,
A whisper of infinity it deafens you.

I was your only friend, we are alone,
Now wolves are baying for my blood.

Lines for Sappho.

Your heart is aflame with that desire,
Those flowers for your Helen of Troy,
Are wilted as you write of a lost lover,
Gone in your imaginations of flowers,
She had wandered Aphrodite's grove,
You had stroked an Aphrodite's buds.

A voice as sweet as flute at dewy dawn,
The music wrapping your beloved's body,
In her white linen robes so pure like desire,
On Lesbos the Muses are singing with joy,
You write a verse of love and lyres do play,
Yet a night still wails the song of loneliness.

I genuflected dumb before the poet's verse.

<u>Two Traditional Haiku.</u>

01

Sun is the fragrance

 Of love breathe that sweet scent
choke

We live in moonlight.

2

Cherry blossom glows

Bright for those it praises we

Weep in a hard frost.

Non-fiction.

Nigel Pearce

New Woman' and Hobgoblins:

The Communist Manifesto in 19th-Century Britain and its literary aftermaths. A Study of Helen Macfarlane and Eleanor Marx.

Positional Quotes.

'A spectre is haunting Europe – the spectre of communism.'
-*Communist Manifesto*, as translated by Samuel
Moore in cooperation with Engels, 1888.

'A frightful hobgoblin stalks throughout Europe. We are
haunted by a ghost, the ghost of Communism.'
-   *Manifesto of the German
    Communist Party*, translated by
Helen Macfarlane, 1850.

'Women are the creatures of an organised tyranny of men,
as the workers are the creatures of an organised tyranny of
idlers … But the one [woman] has nothing to hope from
man, and the other [the worker] has nothing to hope from the
middle class.'
-   *The Women Question from a
    Socialist Point of View*,
    Eleanor
Marx & Edward Aveling 1886.

'If women's liberation is unthinkable without Communism,
then Communism is unthinkable without women's
liberation.'
-   Inessa Armand quoted in
    Sharon Smith (2015), p.1.

'But reality can be seized and penetrated only as a totality,
and only a subject which itself is a totality is capable of this
penetration.'
-   Lukács, Georg *History and
    Class Consciousness.*

'The proletariat cannot liberate itself as a class without
simultaneously abolishing class society as such. For that
reason, its consciousness, the last class consciousness in

the history of mankind, must both lay bare the nature of society and achieve an increasingly inward fusion of theory and practice.'

- Lukács, History and Class

Consciousness,

Abstract.

This thesis I would suggest is of significance because it illuminates an important 'hidden history' of 19th-century 'New Woman' on the British Left employing the methodology of Marxism and its sister models as they developed across time until the late 20th century and into the 21st. It will explore recent studies of Helen Macfarlane and Eleanor Marx, their lives and writing and analyse them from a theoretical perspective rather than understanding them simply as historical figures. Thus, it will recognise the importance of the 'personal as political' but transcend that biographical category. These two women will be shown, like Karl Marx and Frederick Engels, to have been polymaths and will attempt to delineate their demise employing the living tradition in which they had lived. Therefore, it will endeavour to further the knowledge of a uniquely internationalist and revolutionist tradition within Britain and ask why these two women leaders were almost lost to the modern scholar

Contents,

Introduction.

Soundings.

Thesis and methodology. Marx and Engels in Britain during the 1840s and Chartism. Communist Manifesto and its Histories. a) Relationship to The League of the Just. b) Engels' early drafts c) An evolution of Prefaces.

Chapter One.

Kant and Hegel in Britain.

Helen Macfarlane and her translations of Hegel, the Communist Manifesto and other writings including critiques of Carlyle and literary texts. Conclusion: Utopian-Socialism, not Scientific Socialism, somewhat akin to George Elliot's translation of Strauss and Feuerbach and that milieu. No evidence that the two met but were published in contending London papers *The Leader* & *Red Republican*. There is textual material to suggest that Elliot thought Macfarlane too radical. Interestingly they both returned to the dominant ideology of their epoch, Christianity.

Chapter Two.

Death and Resurrection in Nantwich.

Helen Macfarlane's Legacy. Personal tragedies then married a vicar, but the seeds were already there in her earlier written works. So consistent Utopian Socialist /Bourgeois Idealist.

Chapter Three.

Eleanor Marx: A Dreamer of Absolutes.

A 'new wave' of proletarian struggle: the Paris Commune 1870, she writes *Shelley's Socialism.* Bloody Sunday in London, 1880's. Eleanor Marx as the embodiment of Marxist 'praxis'. Conflict with Althusserian R.S.A.

Chapter Four

Ibsen's *Doll's House.* A Study in Patriarchy.

Eleanor Marx was the victim of being unconsciously *interpellated by Patriarchy* so although able to lead worker's' movements she was unable to defy Edward Aveling sexist behaviour and when the class struggle waned her only consolation was the grave. The Althusserian problematic of the epoch would not be answered by the Paris Commune. The silences could only be answered with the symptomatic reading of the narrative that began in 1917. Too late for Eleanor Marx. Eleanor Marx and Aveling claimed to be Ibsenites. At the first English reading of A *Doll's* House given in their Chancery Lane lodgings in 1886. Eleanor read Nora, Aveling (portentously) Helmer and Bernard Shaw, Krogstad.

Chapter Five.

Hot Autumn: Alexandra Kollontai, the Doll's House Unlocked.

Kollontai in the context of the early Russian revolution provided the key to unlock the Doll's House. The Stalinist counter-revolution locked it again.

Conjectures and Reawakening:

Simone de Beauvoir, *The Second Sex.*
Kate Millet, *Sexual Politics,*
Elaine Showalter, *A Literature of Their Own.*
Lise Vogel, *Marxism and the Oppression of Women: Towards a Unitary Theory.*
Sharon Smith, *Women and Socialism.*

Judith Orr, *Marxism and Women's Liberation.*

Conclusion:

 Both Helen Macfarlane and Eleanor Marx were committed, revolutionary socialists. Both in leadership roles. However, in terms of their belief systems, they failed. Helen 'sold out.' Eleanor committed suicide. In *The Myth of Sisyphus* Albert Camus argued: 'The consequences of realization are suicide or recovery.' For these two revolutionaries to have stood on the peaks of class struggle and seen it evaporate would have been overwhelming. Helen Macfarlane sought solace in illusion, her alienated species - being (Feuerbach/Marx/ Freud) religion buried at St. Michael's Church, Baddeley, just outside Nantwich. 'Tussey', ever the active agent, (her motto: 'Always ahead') took her own life, I suggest because, in the 'last instant' her life was revolution and literature and thus because of the downturn in class-struggle and the rise of Aestheticism there was no hope. These women, although significant figures on the Left, were doubly oppressed, by Capital and Patriarchy. I thus, find a degree of explanatory value in 'dual systems theory' school of socialist – feminism. However, a solution can only be found when the proletariat acts as a 'class-for-itself', throws off the bondage of wage slavery and becomes what Lukács, called, the 'identical-subject-object of history.'. As Trotsky noted this is neither a mechanistic nor voluntarist process:

> The progress of a class toward class consciousness, that is, the building of a revolutionary party which leads the proletariat is a complex and a contradictory process. The class itself is not homogeneous. Its different sections arrive at class consciousness by different paths and at different times.[2]

---

[2] Trotsky, Leon, *What Next (*1932)
https://www.marxists.org/archive/trotsky/germany/1932-ger/index.htm

Introduction:

Soundings.

This thesis I maintain is of significance because it illuminates an important 'hidden history' of 19th-century women on the British Left. Their writing and their lives. I will argue that there was little or no intellectual division of labour in the leadership of the Radical Left in nineteenth-century Britain. They were polymaths. So, Marx had been a poet, philosopher, literary critic and economist as well as his political activities. Although this was replicated in both Helen Macfarlane and Eleanor Marx their outcomes were very different from their male counterparts. This begs the question, why? Thus, this thesis is concerned with two leading women figures, their writing and life within the radical left in nineteenth-century Britain. They were not marginalised in their epoch, held leadership roles but became almost lost to the modern reader. My argument is that in order to comprehend this experience a rigorous theoretical structure is necessary, thus a literary material praxis. To return to a quintessential current which runs through my argument is that for those around the leadership on the radical Left in Britain, and later abroad, there was not a division of mental labour between writing and reading of diverse non-fictional and the fictional, the literary. This is exemplified in an eminent study of Karl Marx's reading by S. S. Prawer *Karl Marx and World Literature*[3]. Although I disagree with Prawer when he describes Marx as 'dancing on the superstructure.'. An early love of Karl Marx's had been Prometheus:

> Prometheus is the foremost saint and martyr in the philosopher's calendar.[4]

More significant still was Eleanor Marx's remark that her

---

[3] Prawer, S.S. *Marx and World Literature*. (London, Verso, 2015)
[4] Prawer (2015) p.1.

father: 'was a unique and unrivalled story-teller'.[5] As a young man influenced by those two giants of German Romanticism, Goethe and Schiller, Marx wrote poetry. However, Karl Marx soon rejected 'German Romantic dreaming' for his own Materialist 'reality principle' (Prawer, 2015, p. 17). Marx's 'reality principle' would, of course, develop into a fully-fledged metanarrative held together not by Stalinist heroes nor the exegesis of the precise meaning of this or that text. For as Marx himself famously said: 'I am not a Marxist'. This phrase occurred in a letter of 1890 from Engels to C. Schmidt in Stuttgart in which he recollected Marx's phrase that followed a controversy shortly before Marx died. Marx had written a letter to Eleanor's sister's partner Paul Lafarge and Jules Guesde London, August 5th, 1883 both of whom already claimed to represent "Marxist" principles. Marx accused them of "revolutionary phrase-mongering". Engels continued in the same letter to Schmidt:

> According to the materialist conception of history for a lot of them nowadays, it serves as an excuse for not studying history just as Marx used to say, commenting on the French "Marxists" of the late seventies: "All I know is that I am not a Marxist."[6]

In my search for a method, György Lukács' study into the nature of Marxist dialectics is an invaluable steppingstone although this thesis will also explore the thinking of Louis Althusser and I will note a tension between their perspectives. The former may be described as a 'humanist' reading of 'Hegelian Marxism" and the latter a 'structural' Marxism originating in Semiotics. A third innovatory Marxist thinker, Trotsky, will contribute. All are valuable tools in elucidating 'hidden histories' and the nature of capitalism. Here Lukács is persuasive:

---

[5] Marx and Engels *On Literature and Art. A Selection of Writings*, [eds] L. Baxandall and S. Mora (St.

 Louis, Milwaukee, 1973) p.147.

[6] Marx, Karl & Engels, *Selected Correspondence* (Moscow, Progress Publishers, 1965). p 415.

> Let us assume for the sake of argument that
> recent research had disproved once and for
> all every one of Marx's individual theses...
> Orthodox Marxism, therefore, does not imply
> the uncritical acceptance of the results of
> Marx's investigations. It is not the 'belief' in
> this or that thesis, nor the exegesis of a
> 'sacred' book. On the contrary, orthodoxy
> refers exclusively to method. [7]

Therefore, I am interested in Dialectical Materialism as
a *method*. Firstly, the transformation from a quantitative
to a qualitative condition, thus producing a new state
and secondly Interdependent material opposites which
are by nature

antagonistic, finally 'the negation of the negation' which
creates a new thesis afresh with elements of the old but also
completely new material. I will delineate two core concepts:
1) the Marxist dialectic [Karl Marx never used the term
dialectical materialism]. Engels described it persuasively in
*Dialectics of Nature: Dialectics (The general nature of
dialectics to be developed ...in contrast to metaphysics)* and
2) Historical Materialism. Thus, I agree with the school of
thought which understands Marxism as a 'living tradition' not
a static one as here:

> Marxism is a revolutionary worldview that
> must always struggle for new revelations. Marxism must
> abhor nothing so much as the possibility that it becomes
> congealed in its current form. It is at its best when butting
> heads in self-criticism, and in historical thunder
> and lightning, it retains its strength. [8]

I shall look at the antecedents of *The Communist Manifesto*
beginning with Engels contact with the Chartists and its
histories. Then a) Relationship to The Communist League,
b) Engels' early drafts of *The Principles of Communism,*
1847, c) *The Communist Manifesto* by Marx & Engels, 1848
d) Helen Macfarlane's 1850 translation, e) evolution of

---

[7] Lukacs, Georg *History and Class Consciousness (*Pontypool, The Merlin
Press, 2010). p,1
[8] Luxemburg Rosa *Attributed*.

Prefaces by Marx & Engels 1872 through to Engels' last in 1893.

Chapter One.
Kant and Hegel in Britain.

David Black, a Libertarian Socialist did much to resurrect the figure of Helen Macfarlane in *Helen Macfarlane Red Republican*[9] and *Helen Macfarlane A Feminist, Revolutionary Journalist, and Philosopher in Mid-Nineteenth-Century England* [10]. While Louise Yeoman, a BBC historian has also contributed valuable information.[11] The seeds or contradictions within Helen Macfarlane which led her to move towards Christianity from Left Radicalism were not simply precipitated by the premature and tragic loss of her husband and child. Her consequent marriage to a vicar had its origins in her writings as a radical in 1850. At that time, she was associated with Marx and Engels as well as Ernest Jones and Julian Harney. I will endeavour to show how her translation of the Communist Manifesto was not 'a somewhat fanciful version' as was claimed by David MacLellan *The Communist Manifesto*.[12] Rather it was a work of poetic imagination that was congruent with its host publications the *Democratic Review 1849-1850* and the *Red Republican* and its aspirations which included the publication of poetry. It is significant that David Black uncovered the fact that Heaney cut parts of Helen Macfarlane's translation of the Communist Manifesto in *Red Republican.* However, Black does not provide a convincing reason for this censorship. Unlike most of the leadership of Leftist ''the Charter and something more' Heaney had been a proletarian autodidact and experienced agitator [see Foot, Paul *The Vote* (London, Bookmarks, 2006) pp 89-90.

---

[9] Black, David [ed] *Helen Macfarlane Red Republican* (London, Unkant Publishers, 2014).

[10] Black, David *Helen Macfarlane A Feminist, Revolutionary Journalist, and Philosopher in*
 Mid-Nineteenth Century England (Oxford, Lexington Books, 2004).

[11] https://www.bbc.co.uk/news/uk-scotland-20475989

[12] MacLellan, David [ed] *The Communist Manifesto* (Oxford, Oxford World Classics, 2014). p. xix

Chapter Two.

Death and Resurrection in Nantwich, 1861.

The years 1838-48 saw an upsurge in proletarian activity in Britain and a corresponding increase in interest in both poetry and literature. The defeat of 'the Charter and something more' in England, the revolutions of 1848 in Europe and the cooling of the insurrectionary aspirations of the Irish people all led to defeat for the progressive movement. It was in this context that Helen Macfarlane came to prominence as a revolutionary activist, philosopher as the first published translator of Hegel into English in June 1850 [David Black and Ben Watson [*Radical Philosophy 187(Sept/Oct 2014)]* show conclusively. But it was a contradictory movement, it illustrated 'uneven and combined development' to coin the name of a theory developed by Leon Trotsky which was at the root of many of his diatribes with Stalin and his followers. Talk of uneven development becomes dominant in Trotsky's writings from 1927 onwards when he homed it into a sophisticated instrument to explain the demise of and contradictions within the Chinese revolution of the mid-1920's (see Trotsky, Leon, *Leon Trotsky on China,* Pathfinder,1976.) From this date, whenever the law is mentioned, the claim consistently made for it is that 'the entire history of mankind is governed by the law of uneven development'." (Ian D. Thatcher, "Uneven and combined development", *Revolutionary Russia*, Vol. 4 No. 2, 1991, p. 237.) Although he first developed the theory in *Results and Prospects* (1905) and its explanatory value is of potential use here. Essentially it illustrates how the two motions of the dialectic, quantitive and qualitative can be applied to the uneven development within and between different countries. Also, to cultural phenomena which are not simply reflexive of an epoch but interdependent over the process of history as in his defence of Dante as being a genius in U.S.S.R.,1924. We can see how it was an anathema to Stalin's mechanistic thinking of, for instance, 'socialism in one country'. Helen Macfarlane almost anticipated Trotsky in *Red* Republican, 22nd June 1850.:

> The golden age, sung by the poets and
> prophets of all times and nations, from

> Hesiod and Isaiah to Cervantes and Shelley, *the Paradise* was never lost...this spirit, I say, has descended now upon the multitudes, and has consecrated them to the service of the new – and yet old – religion of Social Democracy.[13]

However, her latent religiosity is there. Not in the reference to the Bible *Isaiah* and Milton *Paradise Lost*. Rather in the registers of 'descended now upon the multitudes' and 'new and yet – old religion of Social Democracy.' At this period in England, Social Democracy referenced one epithet: Revolution. Yet Helen Macfarlane had not thrown off the mantle of Utopian Socialism. She was somewhat akin to Flora Tristan, the French Utopian Socialist, who drove herself into an early grave through exhaustion in her attempts to rouse the French masses to build Workers Palaces. Tristan predated Marx and Engels and they defended her ideas in *The Holy Family*. Helen Macfarlane's incipient Christianity was, I argue, present because of her Idealist reading of Kant and Hegel where unlike Marx she had not 'turned Hegel on his head'. We can understand clearly here in *Red Republican* 20th July 1850:

> Red Republicanism, or democracy, is a protest against the using up of man by man. It is the endeavour to reduce the golden rule of Jesus to practice. Modern democracy is Christianity in a form adapted to the wants of the present age. It is Christianity divested of its mythological
> envelope. It is the idea appearing as pure thought, independent of history and tradition.[14]

---

[13] Macfarlane, Helen, 'Chartism in 1850', *Red Republican*, 22nd June 1850
[14] Howard Morton" (Helen Macfarlane), "Fine Words (Household of otherwise) Butter No Parsnips."
Red Republican, 20 July 1850.

Chapter Three.

Eleanor Marx: A Dreamer of Absolutes.

Of course, people were aware of Eleanor 'Tussey' Marx who was Karl Marx's youngest and most talented daughter. However, it was only with 'second-wave' feminism that she attracted serious academic interest and meaningful studies of Eleanor Marx came to fruition. Firstly, the mould-breaking: Chuschich Tsuzuki *The*

Life of Eleanor Marx,1855-1898: A socialist tragedy, (1967), secondly, an obscure work Ronald Florence (1975). *Marx's Daughters: Eleanor Marx, Rosa Luxemburg, Angelica Balabanoff.* These were followed by what is considered by many to be the authoritative text Yvonne Kapp *Eleanor Marx: A Biography* (2018) which was initially published in the 1970s and took the standard 'line' of the CPGB of its time, revisionism. However, E.P. Thompson wrote a pertinent response in 1976

> But it is not an objective study. The reader who does not like to be manipulated – to be nudged through the evidence towards a prescribed conclusion, now asked to turn his head this way and now ordered to close his eyes, and now shown only an approved portion of the evidence – such a reader will still prefer Chushichi Tsuzuki's ten-year-old biography. Tsuzuki lays out very clearly, and sometimes tersely, the evidence, and invites the reader to form a judgement. Kapp does not. She is wholly entitled to write a very different, and (as she supposes) less 'academic' biography. This will be, for many readers, the virtue of her book. It is, without any pretence, engagingly partisan. She seeks to enter without reserve into the consciousness of her heroine – or hero.[15]

---

[15] https://www.marxists.org › archive › thompson-ep › eleanor-marx "

Indeed, Kapp's massive narrative concludes with the suicide of Eleanor Marx and does not go beyond possibly because of the constraints of being a lifelong member of the CPGB. While Tsuzuki's investigates the circumstances after the suicide with contemporary documents. She finds in a letter from Bernstein to Adler that after the German Party representatives who travelled to England. Upon hearing that Edward Aveling had decided to attend a football match the afternoon after Eleanor's death:

If there was no party interest to take into consideration the people would have torn Aveling to pieces [16]

Then a period of neglect until the next crisis of Capitalism and Rachel Holmes, from a *Left-Feminist* perspective, argued that Eleanor Marx attempted to build a United Front of women and workers *Eleanor Marx: A Life* (2014). This is a useful book because it illuminates much of her subject's interest in literature and culture and convincingly argues that her interest in the Arts was not detached from the proletarian movement. She took literature and drama to the masses. Its flaw is that it drifts towards Left Bourgeois Feminism and attempts to argue that Eleanor Marx held those views which is questionable. She might have believed in a form of dual-systems theory in 1886 when she published *The Woman Question: from a socialist point of view.* However, Lise Vagal argued that was the leading position on the Left following (Engels 1968) August Bebel (1910) and that there was later a different 'line' that emanated from Lenin. 'Lenin criticised the backwardness of many male comrades on this issue..." unfortunately, we may say of many of our comrades 'scratch the surface and a philistine appears.'[17] A Neo-Trotskyist 'line' is pursued by Siobhan Brown[18]. Although it is my sense that these studies tended to err on the personal as political

---

[16] Tsuzuki' (1967) p.321 Bernstein to Adler, 5 April 1898, Adler *Briefuwchsel.*

[17] Vogel, Lise, *Marxism and the Oppression of Women* (Chicago, Haymarket Books,2013),

   p.128.

[18] Brown, Siobhan, *A Rebels Guide to Eleanor Marx* (London, Bookmarks, 2015).

rather than create a theoretical structure for the analysis of Eleanor Marx's contribution to the international socialist movement and her death, valuable though they are.

\

Chapter Four.

Ibsen's *Doll's House.* A Study in Patriarchy.

Eleanor Marx's suicide cannot be explained by simply the metanarratives of Radical Feminism or indeed, Orthodox Marxism. Equally, it stretches congruity to pass it off as Edward Aveling merely being a 'bad apple' who could have driven Karl Marx's most politically engaged daughter to suicide. Nevertheless, Kapp notes:

> The truth is that in moral terms Aveling presented something akin to an   optical illusion: looked at in one light, he could be seen as feckless, happy-go-lucky but fundamentally sound; in another, as an unmitigated scoundrel.[19]

However, I will argue that the circumstances represented a complex conundrum requiring a new reading. It is significant that her mother said she was 'political from top to bottom'[20] Also, Eleanor would quote in a letter to a sister that her father said 'Tussy is me' (Karl Marx quoted by Eleanor Marx to Laura Lafargue, 23 April 1886 (Holmes, 2014, p.251.). While Engels said she: 'was the living and practical realisation of Marx's ideas on the ground' (Alexander (2007). Intriguingly Eleanor

Marx said of herself:

the artistic life is the only life a free woman can live.[21]
It is possible to posit a parallel with Virginia Woolf *A Room of One's Own* here.

Sally Alexander (2007) argues that there was a cult of suicide around middle-class Victorian women social reformers. I shall seek an explanation of greater theoretical capacity in the work of Louis Althusser. Although it is necessary to understand that Althusser was writing in a French intellectual milieu argues Callinicos (2012 pp 267-74).Thus, we cannot ignore Saussure's linguistics, an autonomous system of sign/signifier/signified which was

---

[19] Kapp, Yvonne *Eleanor Marx: A Biography* (2018) Kindle location 7873

[20] Alexander, Sally (2007) Eleanor Marx's Political Legacy- self-sacrifice or self-realisation. *Women's*

   History Review

[21] Kapp, Yvonne, (2018), *Preface*, p iv.

applied to anthropology by Levi-Strauss where he privileges the signifier over the signified, with the latter becoming 'unconscious' and Lucan's Freudianism. One key concept is '*the problematic*' that Althusser described thus: 'the objective internal reference system of its particular themes, the system of questions commanding the answers given.' (Althusser, *For Marx, 1979, p.67n).* By this, he meant an objective structure which allows what can be 'said' or not. As Callinicos describes:

The problematic of a theory is objective: it cannot be reduced to the beliefs of the author of the theory; it is extractable only by means of a symptomatic reading.'[22]

So, as Luke Ferretter (2006, p.35-36) points out some of Sylvia Plath's more violent imagery before her suicide in 1963 could be explained through a symptomatic reading in that she did not have a second wave feminist 'problematic' to answer her writing, it did not exist. As Althusser maintained:

Every ideology must be regarded as a real whole, internally unified by its own problematic, so that it is impossible to extract one element without altering its meaning.[23]

I shall suggest Eleanor Marx's suicide was similar to Sylvia Plath's because she did not have a revolutionary 'problematic' or an alternative system to answer her questions. Thus, a 'symptomatic' reading illustrates the Paris Commune had failed and a new problematic was not formed until October 1917. Hence, in Althusserian terms:

(A symptomatic reading) divulges the undivulged event in the text it reads, and in the same movement relates it to a *different text*, present as a necessary absence of the first.[24]

Also, for Althusser, we are unconsciously interpellated by ideology. It 'hails' us, becomes us we believe it to be ours. Thus, "*Ideology and Ideological State Apparatuses (Notes Towards an Investigation [1970)*" Althusser

---

[22] Alex Callinicos, *Althusser's Marxism (*1976). p, 35.

[23] Althusser, Louis *For Marx,* p, 62.

[24] Althusser and Balibar *Reading Capital* (2009) p.52.

introduced the concepts of Ideological State Apparatuses (ISAs), Repressive State Apparatuses (RSAs), a revisiting of Marx on ideology, and interpellation. In his writing for example, when a police officer shouts (or hails) "Hey, you there!" and an individual turn around and so-to-speak 'answers' the call, he becomes a subject. Althusser argues that this is because the individual has realised that the hailing was addressed at him which makes him the subject. As Althusser argues this is essential for the ideology of bourgeois democracy or, indeed, I shall suggest patriarchy. Further, Althusser maintained, it was required to have a complexified understanding of how the superstructure creates the ideologically necessary prerequisites for the infrastructure to reproduce the conditions of capitalism. It was not possible for the bourgeoisie to rule simply by forced R.S.A.s i.e. the police and army etc. Rather it is necessary if social reproduction is to take place for the proletariat to consent. Hegemony would be achieved, in Althusser's view, by I.S.A.s the churches, media, cultural practices. I would argue that one of the cultural practices that are reproduced is Patriarchy and agree with Althusser that these are reinforced unconsciously by interpellation or 'hailing' as described above. Althusser drew on the work on misrecognition at the 'mirror stage" [stade du miroir] noted by Jacque Lucan in the development of very young children whereby, he argued, the ego was formed. Thus, when combined with Althusser's Neo-Marxism we can understand how the subject may misrecognize socially produced relations as their actual self. Hence my contention here is that although Eleanor Marx had access to both Engels, Origins of the Family, Private Property and the State and August Bebel Women and Socialism they existed in the superstructure as ideological abstractions. These are in a dialectical relationship to the economic base as Marx and Engels had realised:

The ideas of the ruling class are in every epoch the ruling ideas,
i.e. the class, which is the ruling material force of society, is at the same time its ruling intellectual force [...] The ruling ideas are nothing more than the ideal expression of the

dominant material relationships.[25]

In a recollection of a friend, Eleanor Marx showed herself to have been interpellated by Patriarchy ironically in opposition to Ibsen's Nora whom she had admired:

"One alternative," she is reported to have said, "is to leave Edward and live by myself. I can't do that; it would drive him to ruin and wouldn't really help .... It was Edward who really brought out the feminine in me. I was irresistibly drawn to him ... Our tastes were much the same ... We agreed on Socialism. We both loved the theatre... We could work together effectively.[26]

---

[25] Marx, Karl & Engels Frederick *The German Ideology* (London, Lawrence & Wishart, 1982) p, 62.

[26] Aaron Rosebury in Kapp (2018) p,418.

Chapter Five.

Hot Autumn: Alexandra Kollontai, the Doll's House Unlocked.

I nevertheless endeavour to move beyond some of Althusser's entrapping ideological manacles and would argue that in time of severe political and social crisis under capitalism that Lukács is cogent in providing a greater degree of agency and thus transformation:

> As the decisive battle in the class struggle approaches, the power of a true or false theory to accelerate or retard progress grows in proportion. The 'realm of freedom', the end of the 'pre-history of mankind' means precisely that the power of the objectified, reified relations between men begins to revert to man. The closer this process comes to its goal the more urgent it becomes for the proletariat to understand its own historical mission and the more vigorously and directly proletarian class consciousness will determine each of its actions.[27]

Lukács also endeavours to explain why this has not happened by an argument emanating from Marx's commodity fetishism taken to its logical outcome in an advanced capitalist society where the commodity is pervasive, and reification prevents the majority of workers from understanding capitalism as a Totality. However, he argues, the proletariat will become, because of historical 'necessity', "the identical subject-object of history" (Lukács (2010) p 258-59).

However, it is necessary to elucidate both the contents and circumstances of Lukacs *History and Class Consciousness.* He had previously written *The Theory of the Novel* (1916) in which he had noted the decline of writing from the organic unity of Greek Epic to the fragmentation of the modern novel. Lukcas argued this was caused by the

---

[27] Georg Lukács, *History and Class Consciousness*. pp.69-70.

atomisation within capitalism i.e. Ancient Greek society was a Totality while the monopoly-finance Capital of the period was not. Lukcas at this period designated his position as one of a 'Romantic Anti-Capitalist'. 'However, the October Revolution in Russia of 1917 provided him with a solution to his problem. How to remedy the fragmentation of capitalism. In a monumental study written over a period of four years Lukcas not only provided the theoretical architecture to support his claim that the proletariat and ultimately proletarian revolution where the remedy for an alienating and dehumanising capitalism. He also, somewhat remarkably, anticipated the publication of the young Marx's *Economic and Philosophical Manuscripts* which appeared in 1932 with his concepts of Totality and reification. Yet Lukacs was not only prophetic of Marx's claims he also advanced Marxist theory. It should be considered that Lukacs unlike Engels in *Anti-During* and *Dialectics of Nature* understood Marxism as a theory which, at that time, had not the capacity to apply the Dialectic to the Natural Sciences. Rather, for Lukcas, Marxism in *H.C.C.* provides an explanation of the *Antinomies of Bourgeois Thought* and a theory of Proletarian Consciousness as a Totalising force. Lukács endeavours to answer the question 'what is Orthodox Marxism? After the failure of the Second International to organise against the imperialism of WWI and the success of the Third International, (all be it short-lived) in establishing a new model of society based on worker's power and the freedom of the individual when positioned within her social being.

Lukcas wanted to understand why bourgeois philosophy, principally Classical German Philosophy, Immanuel Kant and Hegel had not solved the major problem of philosophy of their epoch, the relationship of the subject to the object, a problem of epistemology. This had manifested itself previously to Kant in the two schools of thought: Rationalists who believed thought was paramount and was a preliminary to the knowledge of the world, if it was possible to know the world. Thus, thought was *a priori* or before to human experience. Manifestations of this school would be pure mathematics and ontological proofs of the existence of God. Alternatively, there were a British school of philosophers especially Locke and Hume who believed human knowledge was *a posteriori* or after experience. Humans are tabula rasa, a blank slate on which experience makes it marks. This is associated with justification that depends on experience or empirical evidence, as with most aspects of science. However, this divide in Western philosophy can be traced to Plato and Aristotle

Immanuel Kant, who was a theist, after reading the sceptic Hume, was minded to solve the subject-object problem. Firstly, he argued, there is a phenomenological world we can see but we cannot know because it is merely that of 'appearances' However, beyond this lies the world of essences we cannot know through the senses he called the noumenal world or 'things-in-themselves'. We cannot know that world like the phenomenological world which consists of 'things-as-they-appear-to-us.' He tried to fuse the two with an a synthetic *a priori*. In order to comprehend that concept, consider these two sets of relations:

a) matters of fact: observed truths, such as 'bread nourishes'.
b) relations of ideas: logical truths, such as 'two plus two equals four.'

Our initial cognisance is that 'relations of ideas' are always *a priori* and 'matters of fact' are always *a posteriori* which was the position held before Kant. Rather what Kant did was that he combined the *a priori with matters of fact* and created a new category in philosophy the *synthetic a priori*. Thus, we can gain some knowledge of the world, 'matters of fact', just by thinking. Had he persuasively solved the subject-object problem? No, argued Lukcas because they were not a synthesis. Not an 'identical subject-object.' Lukács maintained the possibility to know this could only be solved dialectically and thus with a knowledge of Hegelian philosophy and dialectics.

It is of significance to this thesis that Helen Macfarlane was conversant with both the ideas of Immanuel Kant and Hegel:

> To understand Hegel…it is important to be aware that Hegel was writing shortly after the death of Kant. [28]

---

[28] Sullivan, Terry & Gluckstein, Donny *Hegel and Revolution* (London, Bookmarks, 2020) p.24

Indeed, Hegel's concepts of alienation and dialectics were central to both Marx's and, arguably to a lesser extent, Engels understanding of the world. Hegel's *Phenomenology of the Spirit* examines, the unresolved problem of the relationship between the object of the Spirit and of the subject of the Spirit. Unlike Kant, Hegel comprehended the 'Absolute Spirit' as distinct from the transcendental concept of God as a deity. The 'Absolute Spirit', i.e. God, is not separated from the world that it had created. Although, he also argues, the world 'seems to inflict on self-consciousness from without.' The 'Absolute Spirit' rather self-creates both itself and the world until, they achieve a synthesis in what he would later suggest is the Prussian state. Here we can see the divide between the Young or Left Hegelians who concentrated on the process of transformation and Right Hegelians who sought to maintain the status qua. Hegel argued the world is 'the work of the self-consciousness', it is 'the self-consciousness acting on the world' but the world is somehow alien to it. [29] Hence, Hegel developed some terms to attempt to answer Kant's dilemma. Firstly, regarding consciousness as he was not a Materialist rather being an Idealist, 'being-in-itself' which is the object of consciousness or the Spirit and 'being-for itself' which is the subject of consciousness or the Spirit. Therefore, we can ascertain a degree of alienation between object and subject. Hegel's remedy was 'being-in-and-for-itself', the incarnation of the Spirit in the World by Will, specifically in the Germanic State. However, the concept of alienation was developed persuasively by Marx in *Economic and Philosophical Manuscripts* (1844) where he discussed the object of the worker's labour being alienated from him or her, the subject.

How is the movement of the Absolute Spirit self-creation to be explained? Hegel was absolutely clear:

[…] contradiction is at the root of all movement and   life, and it is only so far as it contains a Contradiction that anything moves and has impulse or activity. [30]

---

[29] ibid p.24.
[30] G.W.F. Hegel's *Phenomenology of the Spirit* (Cambridge. 1994) pp. 188. 262.

Here we can understand Hegel's particular philosophical method which was dialectical. Therefore, it is possible to ascertain the Hegelian foundation for both

Lukacs's concepts of Totality and reification. Nevertheless, he would follow Marx in providing a materialist orientation.

Therefore, because the proletariat must ultimately or 'in the last instance' create a Totality which can only be a manifestation of Communism. This is because, for Lukcas, the proletariat has an 'ascribed consciousness'. This he had derived from Weber's concept of ideal 'types. Therefore, although the proletariat as a group of individuals may not seem the class whose 'world-historic mission' it is to create Communism they will as Marx and Engels argued in *The German Ideology* purge themselves 'of the muck of ages' in the process:

> The revolution is necessary, therefore, not only because the ruling class cannot be overthrown in any other way, but also because the class overthrowing it can only in a revolution succeed in ridding itself of all the muck of ages and become fitted to found society anew[31].

Another way of articulating this was by Marx's employment of Hegelian terminology i.e. with a material foundation in the class struggle. Although Marx does not use the phrase 'class-in-itself' directly he does imply it in *The Poverty of Philosophy* where he utilises the term 'class-for-itself'.

> Economic conditions had first transformed the mass of the country into workers. The combination of capital has created for this mass a common situation, common interests. This mass is thus already

---

[31] Karl Marx and Frederick Engels, The German Ideology, in Collected Works, vol. 5 (New York: International Publishers, 1976), p. 53.

a class as against capital but not yet
for itself. In the struggle, of which
we have noted only a few phases,
this mass becomes united, and
constitutes itself as a class for itself.
The interests it defends become
class interests. But the struggle of
class against class is a political
struggle.[32]

The whole of Lukacs methodology is not a variation on
Hegelian Idealism as some claim. Rather we understand
that he was also following Marx as here:

. .. it seems to be correct to begin
with the
real and the concrete, with the real
precondition,
thus, to begin, in economics, ... The
concrete
is concrete because it is the
concentration of
many determinations, hence, unity
of the diverse.
It appears in the process of thinking,
therefore,
as a process of concentration, as a
result not as
a point of departure, even though it
is the point
of departure in reality and hence
also the point
of departure for observation and
conception.[33]

Therefore, we can see how Lukacs amends and develops
Marx's method and then his conception of commodity
fetishism:

---

[32] Marx, Karl *The Poverty of Philosophy* Foreign Languages Publishing
House, 1956, p. 195.

[33] Marx *Grundrisse*. (1973 pp100-101)

as against this, the commodity-
form, and the value-relation of the
products of labour within which it
appears, have absolutely no
connection with the physical nature
of the commodity and the material
relations arising out of this. It is
nothing but the definite social
relation between men themselves
which assumes here, for them, the
fantastic form of a relation between
things. In order, therefore, to find an
analogy we must take flight into the
misty realm of religion. There the
products of the human brain appear
as autonomous figures endowed
with a life of their own, which enter
into relations both with each other
and with the human race. So, it is in
the world of commodities with the
products of men's hands. I call this
the fetishism which attaches itself to
the products of labour as soon as
they are produced as commodities
and is therefore inseparable from
the production of commodities.[34]

Hence, it is clear that Lukacs developed Marx's theory of
commodity fetishism into an advanced model of reification:

'the function of these unmediated
concepts
that have been derived from the
fetishist forms
of objectivity is to make the
phenomena of capitalist
society appear as supra-historical
essences.
The knowledge of the real, objective
nature of a

---

[34]Marx, Karl (*1990*). *Capital*. (London: Penguin Classics). *p. 165.*

phenomenon, the knowledge of its historical
character and the knowledge of its actual function
in the totality of society form, therefore, a
single, undivided act of cognition.[35]

Lukcas developed a sophisticated theory of Historical Materialism and can be compared to Leon Trotsky when he understood that the proletariat is not a mechanistic cog turned by a larger wheel of History. Rather he argued: 'The class consciousness of the proletariat does not develop uniformly throughout the proletariat, parallel to the economic crisis.'[36] Lukcas interest in literary criticism and poetics is of interest because they form a Totality with the philosophy expressed in *History and Class Consciousness* and *Lenin: a study in the unity of his thought*. essentially the same narrative of a 'de-reified' & Totalised proletariat is applied to literature. He employs the ideas of critical realism as a method of distancing himself from the excesses of the 1934 Writers Congress in the U.S.S.R. with its call for a 'Romantic Socialist Realism'. Critical Realism understands both the temporal reality and contradictions of the epoch it is describing but, according to Lukcas it lacks the world-historic overview of Marxism. Lukcas argues the simply using the *form* and *content* Socialist Realism is inadequate. He criticises the Stalinist orthodoxy of the period by appealing to both Marx and Lenin as a defence:

It is no accident that Lenin, like Marx, should regard Tolstoy's realism – in spite of its ideological shortcomings -   as a model of the literature of the future.[37]

Whereas he argues the modernist writer is caught up in his own inner contradictions. Ultimately, for Lukcas a Socialist literature will gestate when the socio-historical are ripe. He did as a mature critic have unrealistically high expectations of Aleksandr Solzhenitsyn

---

[35] Georgi Lukcas (2010) p.14

[36] Lukcas (2010).

[37] Lukcas *The Meaning of Contemporary Realism*

Alexandra Kollontai was a brilliant early Marxist Feminist as is illustrated here in *The Social Basis of the Woman Question:*

> The women's world is divided, just as is the world of men, into two camps: the interests and aspirations of one group bring it close to the bourgeois class, while the other group has close connections to the proletariat, and its claims for liberation encompass a full solution to the woman question. Thus, although both camps follow the general slogan of the "liberation of women," their aims and interests are different. Each of the groups unconsciously takes its starting point from the interests and aspirations of its own class, which gives a specific class colouring to the targets and tasks it sets for itself... however apparently radical the demands of the feminists, one must not lose sight of the fact that the feminists cannot, on account of their class position, fight for that fundamental transformation of society, without which the liberation of women cannot be complete. [38]

Thus, I am inclined to follow Judith Orr *Marxism and Women's Liberation* and Sharon Smith *Women and Socialism who* argue Women's Oppression can only be resolved in a Communist society. We can perceive Nikolai Chernyshevsky *What Is to Be Done* (1863) hero Vera Pavlovna as the successful embodiment of New Woman. [39] Therefore, I am persuaded by Alexandra Kollontai's argument:

> In place of the old individualist and egotistic family, there will rise a universal family of workers, in which all the workers, men and women will be, above all workers, comrades. [40]

---

[38] Alix Holt, Selected Writings of Alexandra Kollontai (Westport, CT: Lawrence Hill & Co., 1977). p. 59.

[39] https://archive.org/details/cu31924096961036

[40] *Alexandra Kollontai* on *Women's Liberation* [ed] Rosenberg, Chanie

Therefore, facilitating the appropriate status of Helen Macfarlane and Eleanor Marx amongst the pantheon of the great international Marxist thinkers and revolutionaries.

(London, Bookmarks, 1977), p.48.

Conjectures and Reawakening.

Simone de Beauvoir, *The Second Sex*.
'One is not born a woman, rather one becomes a woman.'
Kate Millet, Sexual Politics. *Anti-Freud = Phallocentric criticism.*
*"*It is interesting that many women do not recognise themselves as discriminated against; no better proof could be found of the totality of their conditioning."
— Kate Millett, *Sexual Politics*

Elaine Showalter, *A Literature of Their Own:* Gynocentric writing Women's writing by and for women According to Elaine Showalter, argued gynocritics is the study of not only the female as a gender status but also the 'internalized consciousness' of the female. The uncovering of the female subculture and exposition of a female model is the intention of gynocriticism, comprising recognition of a distinct female where a female identity is sought free from the definitions and oppositions.
'In this generation female suicides become conspicuous for the first time; Eleanor Marx, Charlotte Mew, Adela Nicolson and Amy Levy.[41]

Lise Vogel, *Marxism and the Oppression of Women: Towards a Unitary Theory.*

Notes towards an understanding of her work.

1) Dual system theories, which see "two equally powerful motors driving] the development of history: the class struggle and the sex struggle",[42] Vogel set out to construct a unitary theory that transcended the separation of production and reproduction.
2) Socialist feminists tended to argue that women's oppression operates relatively autonomously from capitalist exploitation.

---

[41]Showalter, *Elaine A Literature Of Their Own: British Women Novelists from Brontë to Lessing.*
(London, Virago, Revised Edition 2009) p.109.
[42] Vogel, Lise, 2013, Marxism and the Oppression of Women: Toward a Unitary Theory p. 155-156.

Women's oppression was, for them, located in the sphere of reproduction, exploitation in the sphere of production. In such a dual systems perspective, the struggle against exploitation was regarded as related to but distinct from the struggle for women's liberation.

3) Some socialist feminists went beyond simply identifying these two relatively autonomous spheres of exploitation and oppression, attempting to theorise the relationship between them through analysing the role of women in domestic labour. Margaret Benston in 1969, followed by Peggy Morton in 1971, laid out the basic principles of a materialist analysis of domestic housework. Both understood domestic labour as composed of material activities that result in products consumed within the household. The positive contribution of the domestic labour debate was the insight that the work that women did in the home sustained the household unit and enabled some of its members to go to work each day.

4) Vogel argues that, while the earliest observations made by Benston and Morton that domestic labour produced use values that are consumed within the household proved essentially correct, domestic labour does not produce exchange values, therefore neither does it produce value, nor can it be considered productive or unproductive.

5) Ultimately, despite their intentions, the socialist feminists failed organically to link gender and class, production and reproduction, exploitation and oppression. Vogel attempted to theorise women's oppression while avoiding the pitfalls and limitations inherent in the domestic labour debate. In particular, she formulated her theory by taking up and extending the categories elaborated by Marx in Capital.

6) But, controversially, Vogel also argued that the limitations of socialist feminist theory derived from what has often been seen as a key Marxist work on the question of women's oppression: Frederick Engels's The Origin of the Family, Private Property and the State.

7) For a response to Vogel, See Cliff, Class Struggle and Women's Liberation (London, Bookmarks) 1984, pp 67-109.Vogel criticises Zetkin's focus on women solely as workers, arguing that this makes the wives and daughters of the working class who do not participate in wage labour invisible, she does not engage with the key argument Zetklin was making, namely that female workers gained collective

power as part of the working class as they assumed a role in capitalist production. . Also, Zetkin's argues that working class women and men should unite as their interest is in creating socialism.

8) While many of Vogel's specific criticisms of Engels's text are justified, her overall characterisation of Origin as a "defective text" is unnecessarily dismissive.

9) Engels argued that women's oppression came about at a particular historical juncture; the shift from subsistence to surplus-producing societies. While subsistence societies might be characterised by a division of labour between men, who focused on hunting and fishing, and women, who oversaw gathering and the household, the former did not carry greater importance than the latter. The equal importance accorded to hunting and gathering laid the basis for both men and women's participation in collective decision making. Engels argued that oppressive relationships between men and women were absent in these societies; male supremacy only arose with the rise of class society. In primitive societies men owned the instruments necessary to hunt, fish, cultivate, etc, and therefore when production methods changed and societies began to produce a surplus, it was men who controlled that surplus. In order for men to pass on wealth to descendants, women needed to be tightly controlled. The origin of the monogamous family lay with the development of private property, and, with the advent of monogamous marriage, the nuclear family became the basic economic unit of society. Engels described this as "the world historic defeat of the female sex"; women had become "a mere instrument for the production of children" and were reduced to servitude to men.

10) Vogel argues of Origins, that firstly it misses the significance of the working-class household as an essential social unit, not for the holding of property but for the reproduction of the working class itself. Second, it overlooks the ways in which a material basis for male supremacy is constituted within the proletarian household. And third, it vastly underestimates the variety of ideological and psychological factors that provide a continuing foundation for male supremacy in the working-class family.

11) Engels failed fully to theorise the character of women's oppression under capitalism in Origin—but this was not

Engels's main intention in this work. Engels provides a historical account of the rise of the family as class society develops, rather than specifically setting out to theorise women's oppression under capitalism, arguing that gender roles are social and historical rather than fixed transhistorical entities. Vogel in fact fails to grapple with the historical issue of the origins of women's oppression. Thus, while she correctly argues that the family "is not a timeless universal of human society", she fails to explain why or to explain when the family arose or how its form has changed alongside changes in the mode of production.

12) Vogel's main issue with Origin is its supposed propagation of the dual systems perspective. Vogel accuses Engels of distinguishing between two types of production: first, the production of means of subsistence, and, second, the production of human beings. This theoretical dualism, she argues, ultimately bears responsibility for the dual systems perspectives of socialist feminism. In the offending passage Engels writes:

13) 'According to the materialistic conception, the determining factor in history is, in the final instance, the production and reproduction of immediate life. This, again, is of twofold character: on the one side, the production of the means of existence, of food, clothing and shelter and the tools necessary for that production; on the other side, the production of human beings themselves, the propagation of the species. The social organisation under which the people of a particular historical epoch and a particular country live is determined by both kinds of production: by the stage of development of labour on the one hand and of the family on the other'.[43]

14) Engels's remarks appear to offer authoritative Marxist backing for the socialist feminist movement's focus on the family, sex-divisions of labour, and unpaid domestic work, as well as for its theoretical dualism and its strategic commitment to the autonomous organisation of women.[44]

---

[43] Engels, Frederick *The Origins of the Family, Private Property and the State* , *Lawrence & Wishart 1972, pp120-121.www.marxists.org/archive/marx/works/1884/origin-family/preface.htm*

[44] Vogel, Lise (2010), p.33-34.

15) Firstly, in the US the women's movement was largely composed of cross-class alliances. It had a decidedly different character from the British women's movement, which had a greater orientation on the working class and trade unions or at least to a greater extent., Secondly, Vogel's belief in actual existing socialism having existed in U.S.S.R., China and Cuba rather than a 'degenerated workers state'(Trotsky) or 'bureaucratic state capitalism' (Tony Cliff). Vogel's version of "socialism" has not precipitated the erosion, and eventual abolition, of women's oppression in such societies and, consequently, a distinct movement for women's liberation becomes necessary. Therefore, while repeatedly criticising the tendency of socialist feminists to treat the fight for socialism and women's liberation as autonomous spheres, Vogel ends up advocating a strategy that tacitly replicates this dualism [45]

16) [Marx's] notes suggest that, for Marx, the development of class society and women's oppression are part of the same historical process, but in a somewhat different way than that described later by Engels. . .. For Marx, there had been no "world historic defeat of the female sex." The condition of women in society is and has varied. This is just as true of the time before the introduction of patriarchy as in the period of patriarchy. Instead of seeing this development in a linear way, Marx appears to have been working out a dialectical history of these processes.[46]

Nevertheless, Sharon Smith is absolutely clear and persuasive here:
The revolutionary potential of the working class as it is currently composed has yet to be seen, but it can most certainly be anticipated. When that time comes, working-class women will no doubt take centre stage. [47]

Judith Orr (2015 p,199 & p 220) cogently positioned the ideas of Eleanor Marx in the revolutionary socialist

[45] http://isj.org.uk/lise-vogel-and-the-politics-of-womens-liberation

[46] Brown, Heather. A *Marx on Gender and the Family: A Critical Study* (Chicago: Haymarket Books,

2013), p.134.

[47] Sharon Smith *Women and Socialism,* (Chicago, Haymarket Books, 2015) p.210.

problematic of the October 1917 Russian Revolution. That would have resolved the question of unconscious interpellation by patriarchy in her relationship with Edward Aveling addressed above because as Lenin was to argue: The experience of all liberation movements has shown that the success of a revolution depends on how much the women take part in it. [48]

---

[48] V I Lenin, *The Emancipation of Women* (International Publishers,1984), p60.

Conclusion.

Hence, I have attempted to create a fusion of theory and practice, a literary praxis in this thesis which illustrates both 'hidden histories' of women in the British Left during the 19th century and provides the theoretical apparatus with which to do so. However, conclusively, I locate the demise of both Helen Macfarlane and Eleanor Marx in the failure of the Marxist current within the British proletariat to generalise into the wider working-class movement and thus create the potential for the emancipation of all the oppressed. Because, as Eleanor Marx argued when the engines of proletarian gender and class interests are united:

We are not women arrayed in struggle against men but

workers who are in struggle against the exploiters.[49]

Thus, when the proletariat is united as a 'class-for itself', it would discover its inherent or 'ascribed consciousness' and lead the festival of the oppressed creating 'the-identical-subject-object' of history' (Lukcas), socialism.

---

[49] Eleanor Marx: How Should We Organize?" in Hal Draper, Women and Class, p309.

Appendix 1.

The Communist Manifesto: origins and prefaces and translations.

* Engels first contact with the Chartists was in 1842 when he visited the offices of *The Northern Star.*

* In June 1847 Marx & Engels tentatively joined the League of the Just a largely German Utopian/Christian-communist secret organisation who had believed, initially, in the establishment of 'the kingdom of God on Earth' through revolution or b) utopian commune in America, c) the establishment of worker stock-companies in France & Germany. Marx/Engels were invited to join this somewhat disparate clandestine group. Marx & Engels won the argument after debates culminating in the 10-day First Congress of the Communist League. However, some of the members of the organization persisted in conspiratorial and utopian stances and it was only after the second congress in Autumn 1847 that a recognizable Marxist line was accepted both in theory and practice and the group rejected clandestine activity. Consequently, they asked Marx & Engels to write a political programme. Engels begun work on a document which was a catechism entitled The Principles of Communism in December 1847. However, he was dissatisfied with the document and asked Marx to write a more historical document. As always Marx struggled with focusing on one task at a time but after the Communist League threatened disciplinary action Marx completed the Communist Manifesto in eight weeks in 1848.

* Marx & Engels wrote in the in 1872 Preface to German edition "It was published in English for the first time in 1850 in the Red Republican, London, translated by Miss Helen Macfarlane."

* Marx & Engel speculated in the 1882 Preface to the Russian edition 'Now the question is: can the Russian obshchina [village commune], though greatly undermined, yet a form of

primeval common ownership of land, pass directly to the higher form of Communist common ownership ? Or, on the contrary, must it first pass through the same process of such as constitutes the historical evolution of the West? The only answer to that possible today is this: If the Russian Revolution becomes the signal for a proletarian revolution in the West, so that both complement each other, the present Russian common ownership of land may serve as the starting point for a communist development.

- Engels wrote in 1883 Preface to the German Edition [just after Marx's death on March 14, 1883] 'the basic thought running through the Manifesto remains solely and exclusively with Marx.'.

- In the 1888 Preface to the English edition which became the Standard English Language Version Engels concluded: 'The present translation is by Mr Samuel Moore, the translator of the greater portion of Marx' s Capital. We have revised it in common, and I have added a few notes explanatory of historical allusions.'

- Engels concludes the last Preface he penned in the 1893 Italian edition: 'Today, as in 1300, a new historical era is approaching. Will Italy give us the new Dante, who will mark the hour of birth of this new, proletarian era?'

- The Communist Manifesto contains four sections:
The Communist Manifesto is divided into a preamble and four sections, the last of these a short conclusion. The introduction of the 1888 authorized Samuel Moore/ Engels begins by proclaiming: "A spectre is haunting Europe—the spectre of communism. All the powers of old Europe have entered into a holy alliance to exorcise this spectre". Pointing out that parties everywhere—including those in government and those in the opposition—have flung the "branding reproach of communism" at each other, the authors infer from this that the powers-that-be acknowledge communism to be a power in itself. Subsequently, the introduction

exhorts Communists to openly publish their views and aims, to "meet this nursery tale of the spectre of communism with a manifesto of the party itself".

The first section of the *Manifesto*, "Bourgeois and Proletarians", elucidates the materialist conception of history, that "the history of all hitherto existing society is the history of class struggles". Societies have always taken the form of an oppressed majority exploited under the yoke of an oppressive minority. In capitalism, the industrial working class, or proletariat, engage in class struggle against the owners of the means of production, the bourgeoisie. As before, this struggle will end in a revolution that restructures society, or the "common ruin of the contending classes". The bourgeoisie, through the "constant revolutionising of production [and] uninterrupted disturbance of all social conditions" have emerged as the supreme class in society, displacing all the old powers of feudalism. The bourgeoisie constantly exploits the proletariat for its labour power, creating profit for themselves and accumulating capital. However, in doing so the bourgeoisie serves as "its own grave-diggers"; the proletariat inevitably will become conscious of their own potential and rise to power through revolution, overthrowing the bourgeoisie.

"Proletarians and Communists", the second section, starts by stating the relationship of conscious communists to the rest of the working class. The communists' party will not oppose other working-class parties, but unlike them, it will express the general will and defend the common interests of the world's proletariat as a whole, independent of all nationalities. The section goes on to defend communism from various objections, including claims that it advocates communal prostitution or disincentivises people from working. The section ends by outlining a set of short-term demands—among them a progressive income tax; abolition of inheritances and private property; abolition of child labour; free public education; nationalisation of the means of transport and communication; centralisation of credit via a national bank; expansion of publicly owned land, etc.—the implementation of which would result in the precursor to a stateless and classless society.

The third section, "Socialist and Communist Literature", distinguishes communism from other socialist doctrines prevalent at the time—these being broadly categorised as Reactionary Socialism; Conservative or Bourgeois Socialism; and Critical-Utopian Socialism and Communism. While the degree of reproach toward rival perspectives varies, all are dismissed for advocating reformism and failing to recognise the pre-eminent revolutionary role of the working class. "Position of the Communists in Relation to the Various Opposition Parties", the concluding section of the *Manifesto*, briefly discusses the communist position on struggles in specific countries in the mid-nineteenth century such as France, Switzerland, Poland and Germany, this last being "on the eve of a bourgeois revolution" and predicts that a world revolution will soon follow. It ends by declaring an alliance with the democratic socialists, boldly supporting other communist revolutions and calling for united international proletarian action—"Working Men of All Countries, Unite!".

- **Helen Macfarlane's 1850 translation** is far more poetic using metaphors:
1. 'A frightful hobgoblin stalks throughout Europe. We are haunted by the ghost, the ghost of communism. Macfarlane, David Black notes, uses the language of Hamlet and Scottish folklore. I would argue the first metaphor also rests on her knowledge of Kantian philosophy i.e. the differentiation between the Phenomenological world and the noumenal world or 'things-in-themselves'. We can also note the creative use of metre and repetition.
2. 'Shopocracy' for the petty bourgeoisie. An imaginative Anglicisation which would resonant with British workers.
3. 'Proletarians of the world unite.' Is gender neutral unlike Samuel Moore's 'Working men of the world unite.'

Appendix 2

The Condition of England Novel.

- Writers such as Charles Dickens, Elizabeth Gaskell, Charlotte Brontë and Charles Kingsley 'Alton Locke' based on Thomas Cooper, illuminated contemporary social problems through detailed descriptions of poverty and inequality.

- Elizabeth Gaskell, 'Mary Burton' was Gaskell's first Condition of England Novel, written in 1848 the same year as the Communist Manifesto. It is almost melodramatic and concludes with a working-class assassin and his sister 'the butterfly' being buried in unconsecrated ground. North and South'. A Condition of England question novel written in 1854 is more sophisticated but generically moves between political realism and the sentimental. The genre was derived from an 1839 essay by Thomas Carlyle: 'The Condition of England' in which he lamented the social conditions of the day fearing proletarian revolution. They had indeed been several armed uprisings the year before Carlyle's essay connected to Chartism.

- A problem for these writers was the concluding chapters. How to conclude an exposure of social wrongs with just variants on reform.

- Lukács *The Meaning of Contemporary Realism* is significant as he regarded 'critical realism' i.e. bourgeois writing which understands the 'typicality' rather than the 'topicality' can be equal to or even superior than 'socialist realism' when it deteriorated into verisimilitude or Naturalism.

Appendix 3.

Helen Macfarlane.

- Influenced by German philosophy in particular Kant and Hegel

- Kant on 'the synthetic a priori' in A Critique of Pure Reason that he wrote as a response to reading David Hume in translation. At the time, the 18th century, Western thought was divided between Idealists or Rationalists who believed you could know about something through thought or Reason [knowledge of things without empirical proof they existed] like Descartes: 'Cogito Ergo Sum' = 'I think therefore I am' and those who thought you could not like the Empiricists in Britain like John Locke and David Hume. Who contested that you could have a priori knowledge but rather believed we are born 'Tableau rasa' = 'a blank slate'. Kant attempted to move beyond these competing positions and argued we can know the world 'Synthetic a priori'. To explain this, we need to first understand he thought there was a difference between the 1) the phenomenological world i.e. what we see and 2) the noumenal world which lies beyond appearances. Thus, he had a gap which he attempted to explain. Therefore, some things, he argued, are 'true by definition' or 'Analytic' to use his term e.g. 'men are male' and 'mammals suckle their young.' This type of knowledge we can know without experience by reason or thought in a sentence. Others again to employ Kant's term are 'Synthetic' and requires observation and experience such as 'all lemons are bitter' is based on empirical data he argued. Thus, his 'breakthrough' was some are 'Synthetic a priori' like $7+5=12$ which he claimed we can know by new knowledge. Knowledge about the world by thinking about it. It is a 'Synthetic statement' arrived at by thought which we didn't need to check against observation of the world.

- Helen Macfarlane, I suggest, employs her knowledge of Kantian philosophy and applies it to Scottish folklore in the opening line of The Communist Manifesto to create the metaphor i.e. an image within Kant's noumenal world which lies beyond appearances i.e. **Hobgoblin 'A frightful hobgoblin stalks throughout Europe'.**(Black [ed] 2014 p.119).

* *David Black (2004) p.96 argues that the hobgoblin was both a ghostly apparition emanating from Hamlet and Scottish folklore.*

* Helen Macfarlane concludes her 1850 translation of the Communist Manifesto with '**Let the Proletarians of the world unite.**' (ibid, p149) which is a literal translation. While Samuel Moore advised by Engels concluded their English version in 1888 with 'WORKING MEN OF ALL COUNTRIES, UNITE!''. This translation is the authorised translation by Engels and is the most commonly used version in English. We can see that Macfarlane was more accurate but also did not employ the Patriarchal language of Moore, she thus remained closer to Marx's original text.

* Macfarlane termed the poetic term **'Shopocracy** rather than the usual 'petty bourgeois.

* Macfarlane engaged with other issues of her day. Her first published article in *Democratic Review*, a theoretical journal, in April 1850 was an attack on Thomas Carlyle.

* Macfarlane and Hegel. Macfarlane had not 'turned Hegel on his head' as Marx had done:
  The mystification which the dialectic suffers in Hegel's hands by no means prevents him from presenting its general forms of motion in a comprehensive and conscious manner. With him it is sitting on its head. It must be inverted, in order to discover the rational kernel within the mystical shell.[50]

---

[50] Marx, Karl *'The Afterword'* of the Second Edition of Capital Vol I (Harmondsworth, Penguin Books,
    1976) p.103

- Rather in Macfarlane's thought we can comprehend the philosophical basis in Kant and Hegel for her later retreat from Radical or Scientific Socialism to Anglicanism

Democracy, the Idea of the 19th century, is a great and most welcome fact. This idea has revealed itself at different times, and in different ways. I find it has assumed *four* forms, which, at first sight, are very unlike each other, yet they are only different ways of expressing the same thing, or, to speak strictly, they are the necessary moments in the development, or unfolding, of the idea: and the last of these forms presupposes the foregoing ones – as the fruit presupposes the flower, and that again, the bud. These forms are, the religion taught by the divine Galilean Republican – the reformation of the 16th century – the German philosophy from Emmanuel Kant to Hegel, and the Democracy of our own times.[51]

She was understanding History as the self-conscious unfolding of the Idea as a Hegelian. However, if the Idea was not inverted and given a dialectical materialist grounding, then when the class struggle ebbed the step to an immanent pantheism was the next phase and once made to a belief in a transcendent God although not inevitable was, in the climate of defeat, understandable.

---

[51] Macfarlane, Helen Remarks on the times – Apropos of Certain Passages in No.1 of Thomas

Carlyle's Latter-day Pamphlets *Democratic Review, June 1850*. [Black [ed] 2014). p 5.

Appendix 4.

Julian Harney and Helen Macfarlane, the break and beyond.

Fraternal Democrats.

Fraternal Democrats was an international society, founded at a meeting held in London on September 22. 1845. The society embraced representatives of Left Chartists, German workers and craftsmen – members of the League of the Just – and revolutionary emigrants of other nationalities. During their stay in England in the summer of 1845, Karl Marx and Friedrich Engels helped in preparing for the meeting but did not attend it as they had by then left London. Later they kept in constant touch with the Fraternal Democrats trying to influence the proletarian core of the society, which joined the Communist League in 1847, and through it the Chartist movement. The society ceased its activities in 1853.

- After the failure of revolutions of 1848 Engels claimed, 'the revolution would only be consummated by a new generation of men.'[52]

- Marx rejected the conspiratorial and elitist solutions offered by, for example, Arnold Rouge: '[the people] have no thought for the morrow and must strike all ideas from their mind…the riddle of the future will be solved by a miracle.' [53]

- For an account of the break on December 31st, 1850 at a party hosted by Julian Harney [Marx called him 'Hiphiporah Harney' for his zealous organizing of fund-raising parties.] see Collected Works Vol 10, (2004) pp 626-8.Hearny's wife Mary insulted Helen Macfarlane and Marx blamed him for not allowing her to reply 'and so break with the only collaborator on his sprouting rag who had any original ideas – a rare bird, on his paper.'

- The source for Macfarlane is now Schoyen *The Chartist*

---

[52] *Northern Star*, 4th January 1848.
[53] Marx & Engels *Collected Works Vol 10*, (2004) pp.626-8.

Challenge (1958). She married a man Francis Proust who Black (2004) pp xxix-xxx speculates was mentally ill. They emigrated to South Africa in 1852 he was dropped off in France and the daughter died upon arrival. Two years later Helen is living with an unmarried sister near [200 metres] from where Engels lived with the Burns sisters. She married in 1856 back into her own class in terms of status and education to a widower Rev John Wilkinson Edwards who had graduated from Oxford. Edwards had some 'controversy with 'traditionalists' at his first parish but moved to Nantwich, St-Michael's Baddiley. She died the same age as Flora Tristan, 41 but an Anglican Christian just like Marian Evans George Eliot.

Eric Hobsbawm gets the 1850 translation by Helen Macfarlane totally wrong in his 2012 introduction to the Verso edition. I think he must either have been ill, he died that year, or more likely was he still maintaining the old Stalinist tactic of making the facts fit the line which was Samuel Moore's 1888 translation had become the Standard English Edition after being given the approval of Engels (Marx had died in 1883) and was therefore considered superior . Hobsbawm fabricated an incident where Macfarlane' insulted 'either Marx or Engels'. This was not the case. Julian Harney had organised a fundraiser for the Fraternal Democrats during which Harney's wife insulted Macfarlane' who was not allowed to even the score verbally by Julian Harney. Marx later castigated him over the incident which saw the Red Republican lose the only writer believed was capable of 'independent thought.'.

Appendix 5
Letter to J Bloch, London, 21st September 1890
Frederick Engels.

'According to the materialist conception of history, the ultimately determining element in history is the production and reproduction of real life. Other than this neither Marx nor I have ever asserted. Hence if somebody twists this into saying that the economic element is the only determining one, he transforms that proposition into a meaningless, abstract, senseless phrase. The economic situation is the basis, but the various elements of the superstructure– political forms of the class struggle and its results, to wit: constitutions established by the victorious class after a successful battle, etc., juridical forms, and even the reflexes of all these actual struggles in the brains of the participants, political, juristic, philosophical theories, religious views and their further development into systems of dogmas–also exercise their influence upon the course of the historical struggles and in many cases preponderate in determining their form.'

Appendix 6.
Leon Trotsky on Dante.

If I say that the importance of the Divine Comedy lies in the fact that it gives me an understanding of the state of mind of certain classes in a certain epoch, this means that I transform it into a mere historical document, for, as a work of art, the Divine Comedy must speak in some way to my feelings and moods. Dante's work may act on me in a depressing way, fostering pessimism and despondency in me, or, on the contrary, it may rouse, inspire, encourage me. This is the fundamental relationship between a reader and a work of art. Nobody, of course, forbids a reader to assume the role of a researcher and approach the Divine Comedy as merely an historical document. It is clear, though, that these two approaches are on two different levels, which, though connected, do not overlap. How is it thinkable that there should be not an historical but a directly aesthetic relationship between us and a medieval Italian book? This is explained by the fact that in class society, in spite of all its changeability, there are certain common features. Works of art developed in a medieval Italian city can, we find, affect us too. What does this require? A small thing: it requires that these feelings and moods shall have received such broad, intense, powerful expression as to have raised them above the limitations of the life of those days. Dante was, of course, the product of a certain social milieu. But Dante was a genius. He raised the experience of his epoch to a tremendous artistic height. And if we, while today approaching other works of medieval literature merely as objects of study, approach the Divine Comedy as a source of artistic perception, this happens not because Dante was a Florentine petty bourgeois of the 13th century but, to a considerable extent, in spite of that circumstance. Let us take, for instance, such an elementary psychological feeling as fear of death. This feeling is characteristic not only of man but also of animals. In man it first found simple articulate expression, and later also artistic expression. In different ages, in different social milieu, this expression has changed, that is to say, men have feared death in different ways. And nevertheless, what was said on this score not only by Shakespeare, Byron, Goethe, but also by the Psalmist, can move us.

Leon Trotsky Class and Art: (May 1924).
Delivered: May 9, 1924. Speech during discussion at the Press Department of the Central Committee of the RCP(B) on Party Policy in the Field of Imaginative Literature. Publisher: New Park, London, September 1974, Reprinted from Fourth International of July 1967.

Appendix 7.

Raymond Williams on Gramsci.

The British cultural theorist Raymond Williams notes of Gramsci that this was a huge advance on those critical positions that assumed that ideologies were simply false ideas imposed upon people. Gramsci's analysis, he writes: supposes the existence of something which is truly total … but which is lived at such a depth, which saturates society to such an extent, and which even constitutes the substance and limit of common sense for most people under its sway, that it corresponds to the reality of [their] social experience … If ideology were merely some abstract, imposed set of notions, if our social and political and cultural ideas and assumptions and habits were merely the result of specific manipulation, of a kind of overt training which might be simply ended or withdrawn, then the society would be very much easier to move and to change than in practice it has ever been or is.

Raymond Williams *Problems of Materialism* (London, Verso 1980): p. 37

Appendix 8.

B   Mao on Literature and Art.

In literary and art criticism there are two criteria, the political and the artistic.... There is the political criterion and there is the artistic criterion; what is the relationship between the two? Politics cannot be equated with art, nor can a general world outlook be equated with a method of artistic creation and criticism. We deny not only that there is an abstract and absolutely unchangeable political criterion, but also that there is an abstract and absolutely unchangeable artistic criterion; each class in every class society has its own political and artistic criteria. But all classes in all class societies invariably put the political criterion first and the artistic criterion second.... What we demand is the unity of politics and art, the unity of content and form, the unity of revolutionary political content and the highest possible perfection of artistic form. Works of art, which lack artistic quality, have no force, however progressive they are politically. Therefore, we oppose both works of art with a wrong political viewpoint and the tendency towards the "poster and slogan style" which is correct in political viewpoint but lacking in artistic power. On questions of literature and art we must carry on a struggle on two fronts. "Talks at the Yenan Forum on Literature and Art" (May 1942),

Letting a hundred flowers blossom and a hundred schools of sciences and a flourishing socialist culture in our land. Different forms and styles in art should develop freely and different schools in science should contend freely. We think that it is harmful to the growth of art and science if administrative measures are used to impose one particular style of art or school of thought and to ban another. Questions of right and wrong in the arts and sciences should be settled through free discussion in artistic and scientific circles and through practical work in these fields. They should not be settled in summary fashion.
On the Correct Handling of Contradictions Among the People (February 27, 1957)

Revolutionary culture is a powerful revolutionary weapon for

the broad masses of the people. It prepares the ground ideologically before the revolution comes and is an important, indeed essential, fighting front in the general revolutionary front during the revolution.
"On New Democracy" (January 1940), Selected Works, Vol. II 3.

Bibliography
Primary Sources

Adoratsky. V, *The History of the Communist Manifesto of Marx and Engels*, (New York, International Publishers, 1938).

Bebel, August *Women and Socialism* (New York, Socialist Literature Company.1910).

Black, David [ed] *Helen Macfarlane Red Republican* (London, Unkant Publishers, 2014).

Chernyshevsky, Nikolay, *What is to Be Done, 1888.*
https://archive.org/details/cu31924096961036

Engels, Frederick *Socialism: Utopian and Scientific*
https://www.marxists.org/archive/marx/works/1880/soc-utop/index.htm

Engels, F, *The Origins of the Family, Private Property and The State* (Moscow, Progress Publishers, 1968).

Feuerbach, Ludwig *The Essence of Christianity* (trans) Elliot, George (Dover Philosophical Classics 2008).

Flaubert, Gustave *Madame Bovary* [Eleanor Marx-Aveling translation] Second Norton Critical Edition [ed] Cohen, M, (New York, W.W. Norton & Company, 2005).

Democratic Review 1849-1850 [ed] Julian Harney, (New York, Barnes and Noble, 1968).

Harney Papers [ed] Black, F & Black, R (Assen, Royal Vangorcum Ltd, 1969).
Red Republican and The Friend of the People Vols 1 & 2 1850-1851 [ed] Julian Harney. Reprint with an introduction by John Saville (London, Merlin Press, 1966).

Ibsen, Henrik *A Doll's House and Other Plays* (London, Penguin Classics, 2016).
Hegel, G.W.F. Phenomenology *of the Spirit* (Cambridge.

Cambridge University Press, 1994).

Hobsbawm, Eric [ed] *The Communist Manifesto* (London, Verso, 2012).

Macfarlane, Helen Remarks on the times – Apropos of Certain Passages in No.1 of Thomas Carlyle's Latter-day Pamphlets *Democratic Review, June 1850*. [Black [ed] 2014).

Macfarlane, Helen, 'Chartism in 1850', *Red Republican*, 22nd June 1850.

Howard Morton" (Helen Macfarlane), "Fine Words (Household of otherwise) Butter No Parsnips." *Red Republican*, 20 July 1850.

Macfarlane, Helen The Communist Manifesto, *Red Republican*, [November 1850, 9th, 16th, 23rd & 30th] (London, Merlin Press, 1966).

MacLellan, David [ed]*The Communist Manifesto* (Oxford, Oxford World Classics, 2014).

The Daughters of Marx Selected Correspondence (ed) Olga Merrier & Faith Evans (Harmondsworth, Penguin *Books*, 1984).

Eleanor Marx & Edward Aveling *The Working-Class Movement in America* (London, Swan Sonenshein & Co, 1891).

Eleanor Marx & Edward Aveling *The Women Question from a Socialist Point of View*, 1886.
https://www.marxists.org › archive › eleanor-marx › works › womanq

Marx, Karl *'The Afterword' of the Second Edition of Capital Vol I* (Harmondsworth, Penguin Books, 1976).

Marx & Engels *Collected Works in 50 volumes*. (London, Lawrence & Wishart, 2004).

Marx & Engels *On Literature and Art. A Selection of Writings*, [eds] L. Baxandall and S. Mora (St. Louis,

Milwaukee, 1973)

Marx & Engels, *Selected Correspondence* (Moscow, Progress Publishers, 1965).

Moore, Samuel in cooperation with Engels *The Communist Manifesto* (London, 30th January 1888). https://www.marxists.org/archive/marx/works/1848/communist-manifesto/

Ryazanoff, D *Karl Marx: Man, Thinker and Revolutionist, a Symposium.* (London, Martin Lawrence Limited, 1927).

The Commonweal 1887 (The Official Journal of the Socialist League), (India, Pranava Books Classic Reprints, 2019).

The Commonweal (Journal of the Socialist League). https://www.marxists.org/history/international/social-democracy/commonweal.htm

Socialist League (UK) Archives. http://hdl.handle.net/10622/ARCH01344

The Socialist League Address to the Trade Unions (London. Socialist League Office, 1885, *Socialist Platform Reprints No. 1,* 1977).

The Socialist League Leaflets and Manifestos: An Annotated Checklist (Author) Eugene D. Lemire *International Review of Social History, Vol. 22, No. 1* (1977).

Secondary Sources.
Alexander, Sally (2007) Eleanor Marx's Political Legacy self-sacrifice or self-realisation. *Women's History Review.*

Althusser, Louis, *For Marx* (London, Verso, 1979).
Althusser, Louis, *Ideology and Ideological State Apparatuses (Notes Towards an Investigation [1970)*

Althusser, Louis, *Lenin and Philosophy and other essays* (Delhi, Askari Books 2009).

Althusser and Balibar *Reading Capital* (London, Verso, 2009).

Beauvoir, Simone de *The Second Sex. (London, Vintage Classics, 1997).*

Black, David *Helen Macfarlane A Feminist, Revolutionary Journalist, and Philosopher in Mid-Nineteenth Century England* (Oxford, Lexington Books, 2004).

Black, David, Ben Watson [*Radical Philosophy 187, (Sept/Oct 2014)* Helen Macfarlane https://www.radicalphilosophy.com › article › helen-macfarlan

Brown, Heather A., *Marx on Gender and the Family; A Critical Study* (Chicago, Haymarket Books, 2013).

Brown, Siobhan *A Rebel's Guide to Eleanor Marx* (London, Bookmarks, 2015).

Callinicos, Alex, *Althusser's Marxism,* (London, Pluto Press, 1976).

Callinicos, Alex *Social Theory: A Historical Introduction.* (Cambridge, Polity Press, 2012).

Camus, Albert, *The Myth of Sisyphus* (London, Penguin Great Ideas, 2005).

Carver, Terrell, & Farr, James *The Cambridge Companion to The Communist Manifesto.* (Cambridge, Cambridge University Press, 2015).

Cowling, Mark *The Communist Manifesto New Interpretations* (Cambridge, Edinburgh University Press, 1998).

Draper, Hal, *The Adventures of the Communist Manifesto* (California Centre for Socialist History, 2004).

Ferretter, Luke *Louis Althusser* (London, Routledge, 2006).

Foley, Barbara, *Marxist Literary Criticism Today* (London, Pluto Press, 2019).

Foot, Paul *The Vote* (London, Bookmarks, 2006).

Ginsburgh, Nicola,(2014) http://isj.org.uk/lise-vogel-and-the-politics-of-womens-liberation

Holmes, Rachel *Eleanor Marx A Life*, (London, Bloomsbury, 2014.)

Holt, *Selected Writings of Alexandra Kollontai* (Westport, CT: Lawrence Hill & Co., 1977).

Kapp, Yvonne *Eleanor Marx, A Biography*, (London, Verso, 2018.)

Kollontai, Alexandra *Alexandra Kollontai on Women's Liberation* [ed] Rosenberg, Chanie (London, Bookmarks, 1977).

V I Lenin, *The Emancipation of Women* (International Publishers, 1984).

Lukács, Georg *History and Class Consciousness* (Pontypool, The Merlin Press, 2010).

McLellan, David *Marx before Marxism* (Harmondsworth, Penguin Books, 1970).

Millett, Kate *Sexual Politics, (Urbana and Chicago, University of Illinois Press,* 2000).

Orr, Judith *Marxism and Women's Liberation.* (London, Bookmarks, 2015).

Prawer, S.S. *Karl Marx and World Literature.* (London, Verso, 2015).

Schoyen, A.R. *The Chartist Challenge,* (London, Heinemann, 1958).

Showalter, *Elaine A Literature Of Their Own: British Women Novelists from Brontë to Lessing.* (London, Virago, Revised Edition 2009).

Smith, Sharon *Women and Socialism* (Illinois, Haymarket Books, 2015).

Sullivan, Terry & Gluckstein, Donny *Hegel and Revolution* (London, Bookmarks, 2020).

Ian D. Thatcher, "Uneven and combined development", *Revolutionary Russia*, Vol. 4 No. 2, 1991.

Thompson E.P. (1976).
https://www.marxists.org › archive › thompson-ep › eleanor-marx "

Trotsky, Leon *Class and Art* (Speech, May 9th, 1926).

Trotsky, Leon, *Leon Trotsky on China*, (New York Pathfinder,1976).

Trotsky, Leon *Results and Prospects*
http://www.marxists.org/archive/trotsky/1931/tpr/rp-index.htm

Trotsky, Leon, *What Next (*1932)
https://www.marxists.org/archive/trotsky/germany/1932-ger/index.htm

Tsuzuki, Chuschichi *The Life of Eleanor Marx: A Socialist Tragedy*, (Oxford, Clarendon Press, 1967).

Vogel Lise, *Marxism and the Oppression of Women: Towards a Unitary Theory.*   (Illinois, Haymarket Books, 2013).

Raymond Williams *Problems of Materialism* (London, Verso 1980).

The Economic Malaise: - a Marxist analysis.

'The class consciousness of the proletariat does not develop uniformly
throughout the proletariat, parallel to the economic crisis.'
- György Lukács.

Before the huge expansion of the forces of production under capitalism economic crisis where largely the product of natural catastrophes. However, capitalism has twin demons which means the system goes into crisis periodically and 'accumulation for accumulations sake' (Marx) with the consequences, a climate crisis. Below is a Table which illustrates the three Great Recessions of capitalism: and one of its insoluble problems <u>The Law of the Tendency of the Rate of Profit to Fall</u>.

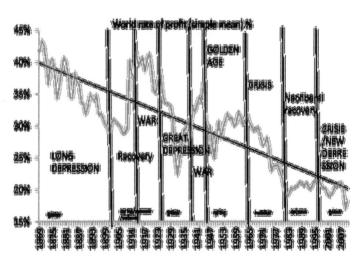

Source: Roberts (2016)

The figure above is self-explanatory as the red line shows the rate of profit over the period of capitalism's development. Michael Roberts (2016, p.9) argues there have been three depressions in modern capitalism, the first was 1873-9, the second 1929-37 and the one which agitates the atmosphere in its repercussions today, 2008-9.

I shall, however, endeavour to explain the causes of and mechanism of TRPF. I am both indebted to the work of two modern Marxists; Chris Harman (who died too young) and Michael Roberts. Karl Marx argued that TRPF was the most significant economic law he discovered. He maintained 'the law of the tendency of the rate of profit to fall' is:

'In every respect the most important law of modern political economy.

- Marx (1973) *Capital vol 3,* p. 748.

Of the many causes of the economic crisis, underconsumption, financial bubbles Marx thought 'the law of the tendency of the rate of profit to fall' was the key to understanding that in the last instant capitalism must create the conditions for its own demise. This theory is amongst economists known as T.R.P.F and it is controversial even within schools of Marxist thought. This controversy has raged almost since the publication first appeared in print of *Volume Three of Capital* in 1894. The argument suggested Chris Harman:

The argument was and is important. For Marx's theory leads to the conclusion that the there is a fundamental, unreformable flaw in capitalism. The rate of profit is the key to capitalists being able to achieve their goal of accumulation. But the more accumulation takes place, the more difficult it is for them make sufficient profit to sustain it.

- Harman (2007) *The rate of profit and the world today*

The lack of absolute clarity in Marx's writing has led to some confusion and this is as Alex Callinicos (2014*) Deciphering Capital* argues partly an epistemological problem. Marx died in 1883 leaving only *Volume One of Capital* in print and his other manuscripts disordered. His lifelong friend Fredrick Engels and his daughter Eleanor Marx put together volumes two and three of Capital and the German Marxist intellectual Karl Kautsky the final volume sometimes knows as *Theories of Surplus Value.* Unfortunately, Marx had died before he completed his last and possibly most important component of the project: ' the book of crisis' Callinicos (2014 p. 57) Alex Callinicos also

argues in (2014) Deciphering Capital that the present crisis was caused by a combination of T.R.P.F, and a 'financial bubble'. So, with these collieries in place I shall not only delineate the foundations of T.R.P.F itself but examine the argument. I shall conclude that capitalism does contain the germ of its own destruction within its very nature, but that this is not mere economic determinism because as Leon Trotsky argued a sophisticated model is necessary:
The proletariat grows and strengthens together with the growth of capitalism... But the day and hour power passes into the hands of the proletariat depend not directly upon the state of the productive forces, but upon the condition of the class struggle, upon the international situation, finally on subjective forces; tradition, initiative, readiness for struggle...
- Cliff (2000) *Marxism at the Millennium*, p. 38.
Let me put some important methodology in place:
In the social production of their existence, men inevitably enter into definite relations, which are independent of their will, namely relations of production appropriate to a given stage in the development of their material forces of production. The totality of these relations of production constitutes the economic structure of society, the real foundation, on which arises a legal and political superstructure and to which correspond definite forms of social consciousness.
Marx (1977) *Early Writings*, p. 425
Therefore, we make our own history, but the circumstances in which we do are not of our choosing, to paraphrase Marx.
The commodity nature of Capitalism is delineated on the very first page of *Capital Vol. 1*:
The wealth of those societies in which the capitalist mode of production prevails, presents itself as "an immense accumulation of commodities," its unit being a single commodity. Our investigation must therefore begin with the analysis of a commodity.
- Marx (1974) *Capital Vol 1,* p.1.
So, what does a commodity consist of? Is it composed of just the investors' money? This is an erroneous view, although as we shall see that is a component. A simple commodity is made up of 'living labour' and 'dead labour', it is the activity of the 'living labour', the foundry worker the

call-centre worker that creates the value. Money does not grow on trees, commodities are made and exchanged for money thus: C-M-C, the commodity does not create the money nor the money the commodity, so what does: 'living labour', the amount of 'socially necessary labour time' that the workers put in to create a good'. 'Socially necessary labour time is here explained by Choonara (2009*)* *Unravelling Capitalism*: There is an obviously objection to Marx's theory, not everyone works as hard.
'Socially necessary labour time' is the labour time needed by a society to produce a commodity with the average degree of skill and intensity prevalent at that time'. It creates a world in which all artistry is removed from work by the application of machinery and the divisions of labour.' [e. g Between mental and physical work]. -

Choonara (2009) *Unravelling Capitalism*, pp. 22-23.
It was Marx's concept of 'socially necessary labour time' that differentiated from and developed David Riccardo's initial 'labour theory of value' which was based on rents and land. Also, Marx didn't spurn Adam Smith's concept of the importance of supply and demand, although he didn't agree with Smith 'hidden hand' or 'price equilibrium'. Both Smith and Ricardo, although significant, were limited by comparison with Marx. So, what is the difference between 'living labour' and 'dead labour'. Another way of expressing these are as 'value': 'variable value' is living labour, the workers and 'constant value' is the machinery, computers, infrastructure etc. We have established where 'value' emanates from 'labour', but what about profit. To use a simple example, suppose a printer produces 10 books a day, each book has a value of fifty pence $10 \times 50p = £5$. However, the worker is only paid for 60% of her or his labour as a wage £3 the other 40%, although created by the worker is siphoned off into 'Surplus Value' which the capitalist will then translate into money = profit. We can see the worker is swindled out of £2 per day, which is generalised to create a rate of profit. This is the dark heart of capitalism, you may think you are doing a fair day's work for a fair day's pay, but you are being exploited in the essence of your being, your work. This can be articulated as an abstraction: humans interact with the Nature in order to transform Nature, and in

this process transform themselves, this is what the young Marx called humanity's 'species being'. As the product of your labour is not yours or your class' but is expropriated by the capitalist, the worker can be seen to be estranged from their work, from their essence. So even in relatively high paid jobs the work is inherently dehumanising under capitalism. Marx encapsulated his theory of alienation, thus: The worker places his life in the object; but now it no longer belongs to him

- Marx (1977) Early Writings, p. 324.

There is another axis in capitalism as well as worker/capitalist one and that is that capitalists are compelled to compete with each other to generate profits to reinvest, to generate profits etc., 'accumulation for accumulation's sake.'(Marx).The anarchy of the market, the ravaging of Nature without sustainability, 'the economics of the madhouse' to quote Chris Harman to the point that many leading scientists believe we are in a new epoch on Earth, the Anthropocene. Where the choice is not as Rosa Luxemburg phrased it: 'Socialism or barbarism.' but rather Socialism or extinction.

There is a consequence for the capitalist of this though he must reinvest in 'dead labour', 'constant capital' in the insane completion with other capitalists. This creates a relationship which Marx called the 'organic composition of capital'. Which he describes in this way:

The composition of capital is to be understood in a twofold sense. On the side of value, it is determined by the proportion in which it is divided into constant capital or value of the means of production, and variable capital or value of labour power, the sum total of wages. On the side of material, as it functions in the process of production, all capital is divided into means of production and living labour power. This latter composition is determined by the relation between the mass of the means of production employed, on the one hand, and the mass of labour necessary for their employment on the other. I call the former the value-composition, the other he technical composition of capital. Between the two there is a strict correlation. To express this, I call the value composition of capital, in so far as it is determined by its technical composition and mirrors the changes of the latter, the organic composition of capital.

Wherever I refer to the composition of capital, without further
qualification, its organic composition is always understood
. -Marx (1974) *Capital Vol 1*, p 574.
Therefore the capitalist must invest 'constant capital', dead
labour' which has the consequence that Marx points out:
The rate of self-expansion of capitalism, or the rate of profit,
being the goal of capitalist production, its fall...appears as a
threat to the capitalist production process...This "testifies to
the merely historical, transitory character of the capitalist
mode of production" and the way that "at a certain stage it
conflicts with its own further development". It showed that
"the real barrier of capitalist production was capital itself. So,
the demise of capitalism is an inherent aspect of itself. So
why is it still here. Trotsky quoted above is a part of the
answer. However, to correct this overproduction of dead
labour, machines, etc. Capitalism must decapitalize or
devalue some capital. We are now beginning to examine
what Marx called the 'countervailing tendencies': 1) Export of
capital, 2) expansion of share capital, 3) extension of credit,
4) reduction of the value of labour power, 5) reduction of the
value of constant capital, 6) spending on arms production,
waste. The problem of capitalism is that although they may
solve the problem in the short-term, they exacerbate it to the
point of global destruction in the long run. There are
essentially two schools of thought amongst orthodox
Marxists a) Some have argued that the rate of profit will tend
to decline in the long term, there will be booms and slumps,
but there will be a long term downward trend, making each
boom shorter than the one before and each slump deeper.
b) Other Marxists believe that the devaluing of capital
restores the rate of profit to its earlier level, these Marxists
see intense crises of restructuring, not an inevitable long-
term decline. The former is closer to reality, but I also
contend that capitalism transforms itself into different modes.
We can see some clear epochs a) Classical Capitalism, b)
The birth of Imperialism, c) 1930's recession and the growth
of State Capitalism, d) the long boom and the 'permanent
arms economy', e) the present crisis. We can say for certain
the crises will reoccur, as Chris Harman argued:

> What matters is to recognise that
> the system has only been able to

survive—and even, spasmodically, grow quite fast for the past three decades—because of its recurrent crises, the increased pressure on workers' conditions and the vast amounts of potential inevitable value that are diverted into waste. It has not been able to return to the "golden age" and it will not be able to do so in future. It may not be in permanent crisis, but it is in a phase of repeated crises from which it cannot escape, and these will necessarily be political and social as well as economic.

Harman (2007).

The rate of profit and the world today has illustrated that there is nothing inevitable about the success of the socialist revolution, but there is about the probability for the conditions of such a revolution to be created paradoxically by the inherent tendencies of capitalism. There has been a recession immediately since Harman wrote *The rate of profit and the world today* and to quote Trotsky *The Transitional Program for Socialist Revolution* in 1938:

> The economic prerequisite for the proletarian revolution has been achieved…the task of the next period…consists in overcoming the contradiction between the maturity of the revolutionary conditions and the immaturity of the proletariat.

-    Trotsky (1977*) The Transitional Program*, pp. 111-114.

Unfortunately, malign Rightist and Fascist forces contest the ideological terrain because as Tony Cliff had argued in 2000: 'The next recession will be like the 1930's in slow motion.'

Bibliography.

Callinicos, A *Deciphering Capital*, (London: Bookmarks.2014).

Choonara, J *Unravelling Capitalism*, (London: Bookmarks, 2007).

Cliff, T, *Marxism at the Millennium*, (London: Bookmarks. 2000).

Harman, C (2007)
http://isj.org.uk/therateofprofitandtheworldtoday/

Marx, K *Capital Vol 1*, (London: Lawrence & Wishart, 1974).

Marx, K, *Capital Vol 3*, (London: Lawrence & Wishart. 1974)

Roberts, M, *The Long Depression*, (Chicago, Haymarket Books, 2016).

Trotsky, L. *The Transitional Program for Socialist Revolution*, (New York,

Pathfinder Press, 1977).

The life and ideas of Emma Goldman.

Emma Goldman was a woman who defied those who would oppress humanity generally and her specific contribution to the rise of revolutionary feminism is today of major significance. Her refusal to submit to the jackboot of any ideology she regarded as tyrannical, whether it was American capitalism or what she regarded as mistakes made by the Russian Marxists around the Kronstadt uprising in 1921, is an inspiration to the downtrodden masses today. But revolutionaries never grow old and as a mature woman of 67 she travelled to Spain in 1936 to help organize the defence of the revolution against the fascists and other agents of international Capital. She was both a theoretician and an activist who wrote some of the most important documents of modern anarchism and also spent time in prison because of her refusal to be silenced. Emma was born into a Jewish family living in Lithuania in 1869. But because of the backlash from the state after the assassination of Tsar Alexander 11 in 1881, there was great political oppression and pogroms against Jews, the family moved to St. Petersburg when Emma was 13. As a consequence of their economic hardship she had to leave school after six months and work in a textiles factory. It was here that Emma was introduced to revolutionary ideas and read a novel by Nikolai Chernyshevsky called: What is to be Done The life and ideas of Emma Goldman. Emma Goldman was a woman who defied those who would oppress humanity generally and her specific contribution to the rise of revolutionary feminism is today of major significance. Her refusal to submit to the jackboot of any ideology she regarded as tyrannical, whether it was American capitalism or what she regarded as mistakes made by the Russian Marxists around the Kronstadt uprising in 1921, is an inspiration to the downtrodden masses today. But revolutionaries never grow old and as a mature woman of 67 she travelled to Spain in 1936 to help organize the defence of the revolution against the fascists and other agents of international Capital. She was both a theoretician and an activist who wrote some of the most important documents of modern anarchism and also spent time in prison because of her refusal to be silenced. Emma was born into a Jewish family living in Lithuania in 1869. But because of the backlash from the state after the assassination of Tsar Alexander 11 in 1881, there was great political oppression and pogroms against Jews, the family moved to St. Petersburg when Emma was 13. As a consequence of their economic hardship she had to leave school after six months and work in a textiles factory. It was here that Emma was introduced to revolutionary ideas and read a novel by Nikolai Chernyshevsky called: What is to be Done in which the heroine Vera becomes a nihilist and lives in a world where there is not any hierarchy in gender relationships and where all work is done on a co-operative basis. These experiences, both emotional and intellectual, would create within Emma a distrust of state authority and a desire for freedom, they created the foundations on which her anarchist politics and philosophy would later be constructed. In 1931 she encapsulated her beliefs succinctly:

"I want freedom, the right to self-expression, everyone's right to beautiful, radiant things".

- Emma Goldman.

By the age of 15 Emma was becoming a lively young woman, her father's response was to get her married, she refused and consequently her parents decided to send her to America. Emma soon realized that the U.S.A. was not the land of opportunity for the masses, but a capitalist system based on exploitation. She married a fellow factory worker and gained U.S. citizenship. Would her life be worn down into dust by capitalist oppression and patriarchy domination? At the age of 20 things were rather bleak, but in 1886 something occurred which would again ignite the fire within Emma. The anarchist movement in the U.S. was quite active at this time and during a clash between militant workers and the police in Chicago, the workers were demanding an eight-hour day, someone threw a bomb into a group of police. Eight anarchists were convicted on very flimsy evidence; the judge even told them they were on trail "because you are anarchists". Four anarchist comrades were hung and became known in working-class history as the Haymarket Martyrs. On the day of the verdict Emma decided to become a revolutionary. Her marriage had not been a success, so Emma now divorced her husband, moved to New York and joined the community of anarchist thinkers and activists. Emma was realizing that:

"It requires less mental energy to condemn than to think".

- Emma Goldman.

She was thinking and contemplating action: Having traced Emma Goldman's early years to the point where she embraced revolutionary anarchism I would now like to examine four areas of her thought: 1) Her commitment to the concept of "propaganda by deed" which had been developed by the anarchist thinker and activist Mikhail Bakunin. 2) Emma's analysis of religion and the failure of Christianity. 3) Goldman and the Bolsheviks. 4) Her ideas on the nature of love. Emma was initially attracted to anarchists of the Bakuninite tendency who were, in the U.S., grouped around Johann Most. She embraced many of Mikhail Bakunin's ideas because he had argued that anarchism was the:

"absolute rejection of every authority including that which sacrifices freedom for the convenience of the state."

-   Mikhail Bakunin.

The position he was arguing for here would not be considered particularly militant in revolutionary circles and formed a basic tenet of anarchist philosophy. However Bakunin's ideas of how to achieve the raising of the consciousness of the oppressed from that of their day to day struggles to that of revolutionary action were radical and are still contested by some anarchists and many Marxists in the anti-capitalist movement today, he argued that:

"we must spread our principles, not with words but with deeds, for this is the most popular, the most potent, and the most irresistible form of propaganda."

- Mikhail Bakunin.

This theory was called "propaganda by deed", it was assumed that a revolutionary act, often of individual violence, would arouse the masses to take place in an insurrection and overthrow the existing order. This was an essential component of Bakunin's political philosophy. He followed this argument to its logical conclusion and perceived the revolutionary's emotions of hostility towards

the system as a manifestation of creativity:
"The passion for destruction is a creative passion".
- Mikhail Bakunin.

The reason Bakunin's position is criticized by most Marxist revolutionaries is because it detaches an individual activist from the collective nature of working-class struggle. These comrades argue that revolutionaries should organize themselves in a revolutionary party within the most advanced sections of the working class and when historical necessity creates the circumstances this "vanguard" should intervene in a decisive way. This party of organized activists will, it is argued, play a leading role in guiding the proletariat towards its "world historic task" (Engels) of creating the "dictatorship of the proletariat", which is the rule of the majority. Once created a "workers state" will, as objective conditions allow, "wither away" (Engels) to leave a classless society. Both anarchists and Marxists believe that the creation of a society without class or gender hierarchies is the desirable conclusion of social transformation. Nevertheless, Emma was, at this time, convinced of the truth of Bakunin's theory of "propaganda by deed". While in New York she met Alexander Berkman, a friend of Johann Most and follower of Bakunin, Emma and Alexander became lovers and would remain life-long friends. This core of three intellectuals was committed to the idea of "propaganda by deed". Goldman and Berkman closely followed a violent strike taking place in 1912 known as the 'Homestead Strike'. The workers had occupied the factory but were expelled by gunmen hired by the owners, several workers died in the struggle. Emma and Alexander were enraged; Goldman gives an account of their feelings (Frick was the manager):
"We were stunned. We saw at once that the time for our manifesto had passed. Words had lost their meaning in the face of innocent blood spilled. Intuitively each felt what was surging in the heart of the other. Sasha [Alexander Berkman] broke the silence, Emma remembered.

> "Frick is the responsible factor in this crime,"
> he said; "he must be made to stand the
> consequences." It was the psychological
> moment for an Attentat (i.e., assassination);
> the whole country was aroused, everybody
> was considering Frick the perpetrator of a

coldblooded murder. A blow aimed at Frick
would re-echo in the poorest hovel, would
call the attention of the whole world to the
real cause behind the Homestead struggle.
It would also strike terror in the enemy's
ranks and make them realize that the
proletariat of America had its avengers".
-Emma Goldman.

Emma then tried, unsuccessfully, to prostitute herself to
raise money to buy a gun, but eventually Berkman carried
out an unsuccessful assassination attempt for which he was
sent to prison for 22 years, being released on parole after 14
years. Berkman had refused to implicate Emma in the
action, and she campaigned for his release. Johann Most,
who had been at the heart of the Bakuninite movement in
the U.S., suddenly changed his position, condemned
Berkman in his newspaper and accused him of creating
sympathy for Flick. Emma continued with her political
activities but was disillusioned with the Bakuninite tactic of
"propaganda by deed". She remained an active agitator and
shared platforms with the I.W.W. (International Workers of
the World) that were an anarcho-syndicalist organization
committed to working class struggle. In 1916 Emma was
arrested for her feminist activities, she was distributing
radical literature to women workers We can see how
Emma's Bakuninite tendencies lead her to make errors in
the tactics to be employed by revolutionaries. But her refusal
to be gagged by the State, patriarchy or capitalist oppression
is something which can be admired today.

Next, I would like to examine Emma Goldman's ideas
about Atheism and Christianity. Her ideas were fine tuned
1913-16. She was to a considerable degree influenced by
Fredrick Nietzsche who she described as a "great mind". His
proclamation that "God was dead" resounded through the
world of all thinking people in the modern period. For
Nietzsche the problem was once there is not a Divine "first
cause" or Creator God for Nature then everything is in
chaos. How can human beings live authentically in these
circumstances? A part of his answer was derived from his
reading of Schopenhauer and the concepts of "appearance"
and "reality". Nietzsche applied these concepts to Greek
culture: the Apollonian seen as the intellectualizing, the

world of "appearances", and the Dionysian as the wild and stormy dimension which is tuned into real life or "reality", the "will-to-life", the creative. It was this "will-to life" that Nietzsche and Goldman believed was being suppressed by Christianity and religion in general. Emma said:

"The Atheists know that life is not fixed, but fluctuating, even as life itself is".

- ## Emma Goldman.

This is her recognition of the life-force, the Dionysian as opposed to Apollonian. That is not to suggest that Goldman was not an intellectual, for she most certainly was, but that she was in touch with the essence of life itself. An illustration of this occurred on an occasion when Emma was dancing and a young comrade took her to one side and said that this was not correct behaviour for an agitator, Emma replied:

"Our cause should not expect me to behave like a nun, the movement should not be turned into a cloister, if it means that, I do not want it".

- Emma Goldman

Of Nietzsche she said: "Nietzsche was not a social theorist, but a poet, a rebel and innovator. His aristocracy was neither of birth or purse; it was of the spirit. In this respect Nietzsche was an anarchist". - Emma Goldman. Her views on political violence underwent a further transformation whilst she was in revolutionary Russia in the early 1920s. Goldman had advocated "propaganda by deed" but had renounced it after the debacle of 1912. However, after that period Emma was still in favour of "defensive" working class violence. In revolutionary Russia, she came to the conclusion that the Bolsheviks had institutionalized political violence and terrorism. Her analysis was: "Such terrorism begets counter-revolution and in turn becomes counter-revolutionary". - Emma Goldman. However, she wrote to Berkman in 1926 that there was only one choice open to people: either to become a Bolshevik or a Tolstoy an (Tolstoy had theorized the "Holy Peasant" as the basic unit of the agrarian anarchy-pacifist commune). Tolstoy had said: 'There is only one permanent revolution and that is a moral one: the regeneration of the inner man". Emma was once asked about her ideas on "free love", she replied: "Free love? As if love is anything but free! Love is free; it can dwell in no other atmosphere". - Emma Goldman. She went on to define her "free love": "My love is sex, but it is devotion, care, patience, friendship, it is all." - Emma Goldman.

Emma Goldman was not a Marxist. Yet she stands with other great woman of the revolutionary current against oppression.

Alice Walker, *The Color Purple.*

Alice Walker argues that her emblematic novel 'The Color Purple:

> '...remains for me a theological work'.
> - Walker, Preface written for the Tenth Anniversary Edition (1992) ix.

Whilst a socialist feminist critique notes that the 'lived experience' of black women is founded on 'triple jeopardy': 'The triple oppression of black women [on the] axis of race, class and gender, through which their subordination and struggle is lived.' - Kaplan, Keeping the Colour in The Color Purple, in Sea Changes, 1986, p181. This analysis will maintain that there is a profound contradiction between the perspective that Walker argues i.e. that 'captive' (Walker/Celia) can be freed by a spiritual 'realization' and a more radical contention that freedom from the dominant ideology of white patriarchal capitalism can only be achieved by social transformation. The latter position is explained by Angela Davis as part of her critique of the limitations of Black Nationalist writing; 'Where cultural representations do not reach out beyond themselves, there is the danger that they will function as the surrogates for activism and that they will constitute both the beginning and the end of practice'. Angela Davis, "Black Nationalism: The Sixties and the Nineties." Black Popular Culture, ed. Gina Dent (Seattle, Wash: Bay Press, 1992), p 324. So, Walker can be perceived as arguing a kind of passivity. The contribution of Louis Althusser theory of 'Ideological state Apparatus' is useful here as it argues we are 'hailed' or 'named' as 'subjects-in-ideology'. by the ISAs. What are the ramifications of this for 'reading text'? 'The subject, therefore, is a social construct, not a natural one. A biological female can have a masculine subjectivity, she can see her place in the world through patriarchal ideology. Similarly, a black person can have a white subjectivity. Literary Theory and Gender: An anthology (1998). p308 But Cara Kaplan points out, once the question of the 'subject' is raised: 'The gendered subject is more rooted in psychological processes, the ideological subject of Althusser in historical and social ones.' ibid. I recognize that a 'positioning' of Walker (1983) in this context leads us back to what Virginia Woolf argued was a specifically' 'feminine' (see Woolf Times Literary Supplement (1923) orientation. Woolf would develop this concept further in her novel To the Lighthouse: 'She imagined how in the champers of mind and heart of the women [where] tablets bearing sacred inscriptions which if one could spell them out, would teach one everything.' - Woolf To the Lighthouse (1927) p 78-9. But a consequence of Woolf's position is that one of the paradoxes within Alice Walker's philosophy of 'Womanism' occurred because it only offers a form of religion as a solution', which Engels argued is: 'The fantastic reflections in people's minds which constitute their daily life, a reflection in which the terrestrial form assumes the form of supernatural forces.' Engels, Anti During in Marx/Engels on Religion (1976) p128 Rather than socio-historical change Walker offers either mysticism or a form of alienation incarnate in the 'American Dream' i.e. Capitalism has the solution to Black people's economic difficulties. Harpo makes; 'Right straight money.' Walker, (1982) p 66. This is highlighted as Walkers' account of 'Celia's firm 'Folkspants Unlimited' is not impacted upon and in the chronology of the story she does mention the 'Wall Street Crash of 1929 and ensuing world historic crisis of capitalism. A close reading will apply this theoretical model and its consequences for the text and Walkers' perspective'. The Color Purple is a masterpiece which broke the mould by bringing Black American Women's writing into the mainstream. But isn't this part of the problem. Let me quote from Simone de Beauvoir the Second Sex (1953); 'A man would never set out to write a book on the peculiar situation of the human male. But if I wish to define myself I must first of all say: 'I am a woman.' Simone de Beauvoir (1953). Walker claims Sojourner Truth, a remarkable ex-slave, who silenced a hostile meeting by exposing her breasts and shouting 'Ain't I a woman' as a 'spiritual ancestor': 'How happy I was when I realized this...I get power from this name that we share.' Walker (1989), Living by the Word p 97-8. A problem with Walker, following de Beauvoir, is that her 'sisterhood' can only be defined by the 'Other' whether it be a Patriarchal God, Man or ultimately Nature as Celia embraces Pantheism; woman is defined by the 'Other'. Sojourner Truth's statement was a rhetorical device which is also used by Walker in her characterization

of Celia throughout the novel to illustrate her growing strength and self-realization from the awful: 'Dear God what is happening to me?' The Color Purple p 3. to the self-assured: Dear Nettie, Well, you know where there's a man, there's trouble.' ibid p 175. Here we see the central 'form of the novel, its written as an 'expository novel' in the form of letters from Celia to 'God' who after her repeated 'rape' by 'Pa'. Celia is the 'focalised character' whom the novel revolves. The first line of the novel: You better not never tell nobody but God. It'd kill your mammy ibid 3. Celia's reply takes the form of a letter; 'Dear God, I am fourteen years old. I am... '. ibid. In this Walker 'contextualizes what become this series of letters. Celia response, alone and frightened, can only be that of the alienated individual crying to God for assistance and the 'woman' being 'interpellated' by the 'Other'. She is obliterated by Patriarchal oppression and the novel will unfold until Celia finally after her two 'realizations: 1) as a woman and 2) as a pantheist which are both facilitated by Shug and Celia can say:
'Amen.' (So be it). ibid 261 Hence Walker is consistent in her use of 'theological' idiom.

The 'point of view employed by Walker is therefore appropriately a 'first person narrator' technique. Celia is the central 'narrator', but her sister Nettle is sometimes, and this provides an atmosphere of intimacy congruent with Walker's concept of 'Womanism'. Hence the 'reader 'has a sympathetic, almost empathetic, relationship to the protagonist Celia and her sister Nettle who is the' minor character'. This 'first person narration' method aspires to creating a sense of 'authenticity' which Walker achieves in Celia. Celia refers to herself in the 'first-person singular. It is important that Walker, the author, should not be regarded as the 'narrator', a technique used by Walker to articulate her concept of 'Womanism''
'Us sleep like sister me and Shug.' ibid p 131. Employing the alliterative repeating of's' sounds which is onomatopoetic, it sounds like 'Sisterhood' with a warm and full resonance. but there is also an element of phonoaesthetic i.e. relating sound and meaning by association. Here the monosyllable us' followed by 'Shug' are related: '.... Hugging is good. Snuggle. All of its good.' ibid. Here Walker employs assonance with the '[H]u' and '[Sn] u again creating a domed

rather than 'phallic' sound representative of Celia first 'realization of the 'Divine not being distinct' (Walker Preface) through Shug; lesbianism. Celia's second and concomitant 'realization' of the 'Divine being separate' also is derived from Shug who is a symbol of 'independent womanhood'. Walker uses a short and piece of 'dialogue' as a prelude to this 'epiphany', almost like: 'The Dark Night of the Soul' described so eloquently by St John of the Cross (1968). 'Dear Nettie, I don't write to god no more... what happened to god? ast Shug. Who that? I say ... She talk and talk and try to bulge me from blasphemy. but I blaspheme as much as I want to.' ' ibid p174. But Shug enlightens her as this animated dialogue, a discourse of black women discovering Divinity in their Image. '... one things in the white folks bible. Shug! I say God wrote the Bible it had nothing to do with white folks ... When I found out god was a man and white I lost interest.' ibid p 175. Shug continues: Yeah, It, god ain't a he or She it's an It. ibid p 176. Then Shug provides the revelation:

'It pisses God off if you walk past by the color purple and don't notice it.' ibid p 177. Hence the 'double realization' achieves fruition; 'sisterhood' and Pantheism'. Walker has used a genre similar to 'melodrama' with a reliance on Jungian 'synchronicity' to articulate her ideology of 'Womanism' and it broke the mould. Elaine Showalter uses a term: 'geocentricism' to describe a framework of 'women's production, motivation and analysis '

Finally, I would agree with Eagleton that: For Marx, 'then, the ability of art to manifest human power is dependent on the moment of History itself.' Eagleton, (1976) p68. The epoch The Color Purple was written in meant it could not act as a catalyst for revolution but was appropriated by the 'Ideological State Apparatus'. Althusser: 'The mirror structure of ideology ensues: 1. The absolute guarantee that everything is real is as so... everything will be alright: Amen 'So be it.' Literary Theory: an anthology (1998) p 302.

Bibliography

Davis, A (1992) Black Nationalism: The Sixties and The Nineties in Black popular Culture, ed Gina Dent, Bay Press.

de Beauvoir, S (1953) 'Introduction', The Second Sex, Pan Books.

Eagleton, T (1976) Marxism and Literary Criticism, Routledge.

Engels, F (1878) Anti-During in' Marx and Engels: On Religion', Progress Publications, Moscow.

Kaplan, C (1986) Keeping the Colour in The Color Purple in, Sea Changes: Essays on Culture and Feminism, Verso.

John of the Cross (1968) The poems of St. John of the Cross, New Directions Paperbook.

Rivkin, J and Ryan, M (eds) (1998) Literary Theory: an anthology, Blackwell.

Walker, A (1998) Living by the Word, Mariner Books.

. Walker, A (1983) The Color Purple, The Woman's Press.

Walker, A (1993) Preface written for the Tenth Anniversary, The Woman's Press.

Woolf, V (1923) Times Literary Supplement.

Woolf, V (1927) To the Lighthouse, Vintage.

On Byron Childe Harold's *Pilgrimage Canto IV* and John Keats' '*Ode to a Grecian Urn'*.

'Two souls, alas! are lodged within my breast, which struggle there for undivided reign: One to the world, with obstinate desire, Above the mist the other doth aspire, with sacred vehemence, to purer spheres'. Goethe (1999) Faust 1 ii 40-43.

My analysis will argue that the dialectic delineated by Goethe in 1776-7 which is contained within the individual can be understood as a commentary on Romanticism and can be seen as central to the themes of 'loss and the past' manifest in British Hellenism. This thesis will then be applied to Byron and Keats by 'close reading'. 'This doubleness – poetry-in-itself v. poetry – for – itself and beyond – it - self – is written into Romantic aspiration.' Chandler and McLane (2008) p 7. Sartre concept of 'being – in – itself v being – for – itself' (see Warnock 1965 p 61-2) i.e. 'being –in—itself' has a 'essence', it is real in itself while 'being – for –itself' only exists as far as it goes beyond it-self into 'nothingness'. These concepts are usefully employed here to illustrate the dualism between 'world' and 'pure spheres' and indeed to the nature of the two poems. Byron's Childe Harold's Pilgrimage is understood as existing 'in-itself', the Byronic is anti – Hero is condemned to wander 'in-itself'. Byron is here commenting on Don Juan but it is true of the 'Byronic Hero' generally: 'Almost all is real life, either my own or people I know.' Wu (1998) p 664. While Keats Ode to a Grecian Urn' is 'for-itself' it transcends it-self into a 'nothingness because as Keats explains in his theory of 'negative capability': 'It is not itself- it has no self – it has everything and nothing.' Owen and Johnston (1998) p 1042. 'It has as much delight in conceiving an Iago as an Imogen.' ibid and therefore in: Ode to a Grecian Urn: 'Beauty is truth, truth beauty…' l 49. ibid. p 396. It is 'beyond - itself'. These poems, therefore, represent a tension between 'essence' and 'existence', Hence they inherently comment on the theme of lose and the past which is rooted in these questions. A fascination with the Greek in relation to the past and present as well as the nature of the imagination was central to the 'second generation' of British Romantic poets:
'The common interest to all varieties of Romantic Hellenism

was an interest in Greece or the Grecian model and a desire to appropriate it to present purpose... this interest was sometimes negative, and sometimes positive, sometimes as a nostalgic yearning, sometimes radical, sometimes conservative.' Ward (1993) p 150.

I shall now examine the relationship of poetic form to the 'past' and 'loss' in the context of my argument in relation to Byron 'Childe Harold's Pilgrimage'. In its title the word 'Childe' is a reference to medieval knights' of noble birth. and suggests a sense of continuity with the past. The selection of Spenserian stanzas alludes to Spencer: 'Fairy Queen' and is subtitled 'A Romaunt'. Both have a resonance with an 'idealized' past, but immediately the poem turns to contemporary themes. The poem exists in-itself, it is itself and nothing else. The body of the work Cantos IV Stanzas 139-144 will now be analysed by a 'close reading'. The general structure of Canto IV is Spenserian stanza rhyming: ABABBCBCC with eight iambic pentameters although these can be irregular followed by a longer alexandrine line The Canto IV announces, almost declaims: u / u / u / u / u / 'And here the buzz of eager nations ran,' IV 139: 1143. Owens and Johnson. (1998). p 249 This scans as an iambic pentameter. The rhythm and choice of the verbs 'buzz' and 'eager' to describe the noun 'nations' is declamatory. We are immediately told that the question of 'nations' will be addressed. In the next line the effect of the use of a Caesura in this sentence makes it apparent that this is not going to be poem applauding the status quo of his day. We will see how this develops into a narrative of the Might and the fall of Rome; itself a biblical narrative of impending catastrophe 'In murmured pity, or loud-roared applause,' IV: 139. 1144 ibid That it is a poem of unresolved dialectical contradictions but is 'for itself' i.e. it is what it is. The line is enhanced by the use in the first half of assonance: with the sounds: 'ur', 'ur' 'e'. These are quite sounding, as is appropriate for pity. The second half in contrast is onomatopoeic; it is the sound of reactionary Nationalism which Byron detested. He then universalizes this theme with a clever combination: 'What matters where we fall to fill the maws IV: 1250. Of worms - on battle-plains or listed sport?' IV: 1251. Several components of these lines are useful to our understanding both of meaning and the devices used to achieve them. The narrator is asking a fundamental question: 'What does it matters when and where and how we die?' How does Byron employ poetic devices to achieve this? The pace of the line 1250 speeds up with the last three iambic feet enhanced by the enjambment into 'of worms' i.e. death line 1251. The reader feels an immediacy of mortality. With 'maws' suggesting 'devouring' or 'greedy' the reader understands that the narrator is speaking of the end rather than any form of transcendence, it is 'poetry – in - itself.' Here we can perceive a complex interweaving of fundamental themes of loss and the past and the nature of the poetic imagination. The reader is now taken on a journey through the rise and fall of Rome: 'A ruin, yet what a ruin! IV: 1279. The repetition of the word 'ruin' combined with an exclamation mark creates a powerful sound to accompany a potent idea. 'The Roman model was again a two-edged sword: splendid and glorious but condemned to fall...Rome was then juxtaposition...of the pure with the savage.' Groom (2008). p 49. This juxtaposition is present in Childe Harold's Pilgrimage as 'life or death', 'revolution or reaction' and with loss and the past. the poem does transcend it-self, it is 'for-itself'.

Turgenev: *Fathers and Sons*. **Notes on Realism in literature**.

' This analysis argues that although literary 'form' is determined by the socio-economic conditions i.e. form is determined by the content it embodies and as the social 'mode of production' changes the nature of that 'content' is transformed and therefore effects the 'form'(see Eagleton (1976). That there is not a 'reflex' connection between them and that by examining the way 'form' is used in Fathers and Sons' (1863), in the light of the modern Realist novel developed by Lukcas. We can comprehend how Realist and non-Realist techniques achieve a 'totality'. I shall argue that Marx (1859) constructs a persuasive theoretical model which can be applied to the Realist Novel. However this must be understood in the context of a 'dialectical' relationship between 'form' and 'content' Hegel (1831). Having applied Lukcas' model to Turgenev (1863) especially his ideas of 'typicality' (by this he means an individualized character combined with a 'world historic' epoch, 'world historic' can defined as a 'progressive' historical epoch e.g. the period in Russia during 1860's) and I argue that because Bazarov was both a 'typical' and 'world historic' character and therefore the novel achieves a 'totality' i.e. a 'balance of 'general and particular and also the conceptual and sensuous' (Eagleton 1976). Was he prime 'New Man in the Realist Novel? I contest this with reference to Turgenev Hamlet and Quixotic (1860). Consequently we can comprehend the roots of the decline of the Realist Novel into both Naturalism and into Formalism with the concomitant rise of 'irrationalism' Lukcas(1938).I argue that this degeneration originated from the 'idea' of 'the superfluous man' Turgenev (1850) in Russian literature which itself was the product of material conditions. I will illustrate these claims by close reference to the text and in particular contrasting Realist and non-Realist literary techniques. Clear socio-economic forces influenced the 19th century Realist novel a) the convolutions caused in Western Europe would spread West b) the defeat of Imperial Russia in the Crimean War (1853-6) and the rise of the razanochinets new class of educated young men and women who were not aligned with the ruling class and estranged from the 'traditions' and who acted on their beliefs. this concept found its highest

manifestation in 'What is to be Done? Chernyshevsky:
(1863). Fathers and Sons is composed of both Realist and
non-Realist elements. It's not a political trait that is
masquerading as a Realist model and confined by the
dictates 'socialist Realism as in 'Mother: Gorky (1903) nor is
it t an example of 'genre' of another form of distorted Realist
form such as 'the Naturalism of Zola in 'Germinal': 'By
naturalism Lukcas means the distortion of realism which
merely photographs the surface phenomena of society
without penetrating to their significant essences.' Eagleton
(1976) p 28. Turgenev employs some basic Realist
methods, at the beginning of the book we are introduced to
an 'Omniscient Narrator who can describe the 'plot' but also,
significantly see into the 'essences', the 'totalities' that
Lukcas maintains is the central aspect of Realism; If a writer
strives to represent reality as it truly is, i.e. if he is an
authentic realist, then the question of totality plays ad
decisive role. ibid. Turgenev immediately acquaints us with
an omniscient narrator i.e. who both describes and sees
beyond the surface: 'We will acquaint the reader with him
'His name is Nicolai Petrovich Korsakov. Turgenev (1863) p
1. This is immediately 'counter-balanced' by an account of
the Korsakov's own account of his life as both social history
in which we are given unique access to his character not as
the product dialogue but all-seeing narrator; portentously we
are told:: but then along came 1848' ibid p. 5. The year
which revolutions swept Europe. Soon this ere is a
connecting passage of 'dialogue' which also has the quality
of 'showing' 'Dad let me introduce my good friend
Bazarov....' 'Sincerely glad, 'h began, and grateful to you for
kindly intending to stay with us...Permit me to ask your
name...' 'Evegeny Vasilev' Bazarov answered in a lazy but
manly voice.' ibid p.7. This is an example of both Turgenev's
ability to combine Realist technique and aspects of his 'style'
in this dialogue, it is an apparently straightforward piece of
Realism but an 'atmosphere' is being created: 'As a conjurer
of atmosphere Turgenev had no equal.' Freeborn (2001). p.
105. I would argue that 'atmosphere is similar to 'essence';
Turgenev has looked beyond the objective 'material reality'
in a fashion 'typical' of Realist technique, indeed here is
employing a technique used by Austin of 'polarized
characters' e.g. Elizabeth and Mrs Bennett. However I would

suggest that Turgenev's characters to do possess that opposition of and 'roundness' and 'flatness respectively found in the Austin's two mentioned. They are character in a seminal example of the Realist genre in Pride and Prejudice Austin (1818). But in the 19th century Realist novel, the characters and in particular Bazarov transcend this. They develop in the context of their societal circumstances i.e. in the 'content' but the unique 'form' then rebounds to transform the 'content' which, in turn affects the socio-economic conditions from which it has arisen. While juxtaposing Austin and Turgenev it is of interest to examine Freeborn a comment made by Freeborn regarding Turgenev: 'he succeeded in creating the world of the ... country estate so perfectly that no other writer has surpassed him.' Freeborn (2001) This is significant in several ways, firstly Freeborn is suggesting the great technical skill in 'showing' and 'telling' to produce the 'totality' of the country estate and secondly the importance of this 'setting' in Turgenev (1863) because of the physical limitations he imposed the characters are is using the technique of 'concentration' in which he characters emotions are intensified and they experience a number of realizations. An example of this is Chapter 17; Odintosva is talking about her life with Bazarov in her 'country estate'. was firstly provided with an example 'telling' by the narrator, this is a fundamental Realist Technique: 'The estate where Anna Sergeevna lived stood on a bare sloping hill a short distance from a yellow stone church with a green roof and white pillars' Turgenev (1883) p 81. I shall attempt to illustrate firstly the complex relationship between 'content' and 'form' 'The work of the German left-wing Hegelian whose Essence of Christianity (1841) had a major impact in Russia in the 1840's embraced a materialist outlook.' Oxford (2009) p129 Hence the 'social context of Turgenev (1883) influence its 'content' which acted the 'form' and its automatons development: 'Art possess a high degree of autonomy.' Trotsky (1924) Baranov's crude Materialism emanates from Feuerbach (1841): He addresses Odintosva: 'You're healthy, independent and wealthy-what more could you want?'' 'What do I want...yes, I'm old...and ahead of me a long, long road with nothing to aim for...I just don't want to go down it.' 'You're disillusioned.' Turgenev (1883) p. 97/8.

Two main aspects of Turgenev's technique are illustrated here 1) the use of dialogue as a means to create characterization but 2) this is an epiphany for both characters a) Baranov begins to see the constraints of pre-Marxist Materialism, b) Odintosva experiences an 'existential crisis' and they both realize they share an estrangement from Russian society and, indeed, the natural world. We can understand how on page 81+97/8 Turgenev uses the 'conjuncture' of 'telling' followed by 'dialogue' to create this moment of realization. The main emphasis of 'focalization' in Fathers and Sons is on Baranov because he is 'the centre of consciousnesses of the narrative. Bazarov is an example of Turgenev's complex characterization a): he a fictional figure and b) a figure based on a young doctor Turgenev had met and c) a 'typical' character. In 'Studies in European Realism (1972) and The Historical Novel (1962) Lukcas explained his ideas on the Realist novel. As I have illustrated Bazarov embodied what Lukcas called 'typical' character which must live in a 'World Historic' epoch' without being submerged in them and is therefore 'individualized. I would argue that the 1860's as such a period. For Lukcas what created a great realist novelist was not individual ability but: 'the richness and profundity of created characters relies upon the richness and profundity of the social process.' New Hungarian Quarterly (Autumn 1972) Finally, Turgenev although a great Realist writer derived much from non-realist sources and applied then in his novels. In Hamlet and Don Queitite (1860) they are seen as opposite poles; one introspective, the other lives outside of his psyche and is capable of self-sacrifice This is an non-realist model constructed above, and shows Turgenev' flaw, his 'superfluous man' (1850) who has radical words but no action can be seen in Bazarov while the prototype for the Bolsheviks would be Chernyshevsky (1863) heroine Vera Pavlovna. Turgenev was not: 'On the threshold of the future' Turgenev: (Oxford 2001) p 132. We can comprehend the roots of the decline of the Realist Novel into both Naturalism Lukcas (1938) an originating in the non-Realist' of 'the superfluous man' Turgenev (1850).

Bibliography

Austin, J Pride and Prejudice (1813) Oxford World Classics.
Chernyshevsky (1863) in ed Cornwael I Routledge Guide to Russian Literature Routledge.
Eagleton, T (1989) Marxism and Literary Criticism Routledge.
Freeborn The Classic Russian Novel in Cornwell, I ed The Routledge guide to Russian Literature. Routledge
Hegel, F. (1831) Philosophy of Fine Art in Eagleton (1989) Marxism and literary Criticism Routledge
Lukcas. (1971) The Theory of the Novel London in Eagleton, T (1989) Marxism and literary Criticism Routledge.
Marx, K, (1977) Selected Works OUP.
New Hungarian Quarterly Autumn 1972.
Oxford Nineteenth Century Thought and Literature in Cornwell, I ed The Routledge Guide to Russian Literature Routledge.

Prose-fiction.

The Cave.

The unexamined existence is all right for cattle, but not for human beings.'

-

Socrates.

'Those who do not move do not notice their chains.'
                                        - Rosa Luxemburg.

1.

The winds whirled around the mountains and they chilled cruelly. It was another long day of captivity for those in the Cave, shackled to the ridges and hollows of the inner wall. These both cut into the flesh and it created the discomfort of bending to attempt to create some kind of ease for rest. A fire of wood undulating, almost pulsating with bright yellow flames and then heaving embers cast their shadows. They had been enslaved for a very long duration and, no one was quite sure amongst either the prisoners or guards for how long?

The superintendent would only visit very occasionally but would always utter wise and high-flouting words, This did not ameliorate the circumstances of either the captives or their captors. Of course, all were stranded in a Cave halfway up a mountain and all they wanted was freedom. They had even forgotten how they came to be in this wretched Cave, but they were aware that the superintendent knew or at least that was the impression he gave with his protracted philosophical monologues. They could only be soliloquies not just because he was the superintendent but as no one else could understand, but one or two were beginning to get his general drift under the influence of a fellow prisoner. Something bout shadows and how these were illusions but that it what we saw we knew for certain. As we were chained face forward to the cave wall and the fire was behind it any man or woman could deduce, they were shadows. I can tell you the chains were real enough and the shackles and the gruel thick or thin that was our cuisine. For that matter those from the Elite Guard, handpicked to be our guards did not have a qualitatively different diet. In fact, we were all, if they could but understand, all the victims of the superintendent's obsession, his thought-experiment. However, I thought while we were stuck halfway up a mountain in a bloody Cave, bound by iron to the cave wall, great...the wonders of the Athenian State.

2.

My discontent was beginning to be shared by some of the other slaves, not in the form of speech but by any number of hardly discernible acts of defiance; a bowl of gruel refused here, a refusal to stand there. Nothing that overtly the startled the guards because they were almost like somnambulists with the boredom of work and they thought in Formal Logic and we did in dialectics. Not what in thousands of years would be termed 'dialectical materialism' and 'historical materialism'. After all, would not Frederick Engels write in Anti-During.' The ancient Greek philosophers were all natural-born dialecticians and Aristotle, the most encyclopaedic intellect among them, had even already analysed the most essential forms of dialectical thought." Engels would develop this further, again in *Anti-During*, 'For dialectical philosophy nothing is final, absolute, sacred. It reveals the transitory character of everything and in everything: nothing can endure before it except the uninterrupted process of becoming and passing away, of endless ascendancy from the lower to the higher."

So now you see me as I am unfrocked, the scholar activist who lives and has always been present since those first hesitant incantations which would poetry and, later, prose. There will be tectonic shifts in the world called revolutions and then as noted by V. I. Lenin relations would one day be transformed: "antagonism and contradiction are utterly different. Under socialism antagonism disappears, but contradiction remains." (Critical Notes on Bukharin's Economics of the Transition Period)' Meanwhile back in our Cave the temperature was beginning to rise.

3.

What was this? Animal fat to ease the abrasion of our irons. So, some ethical considerations are being included as a variable in the great experiment. But the stench and now the guards are beginning to feel their status is being undermined by no one less than the superintendent, the philosopher Plato, pupil of Socrates of the subversion of the youth and the State enforced hemlock draft drunk to death.

But what of this philosopher elite, or are we just but "cattle" to be cast in caves to proof some theory of Forms? Remember reader they used cattle trucks to take firstly, the psychiatric patients with black triangles. then the Left with Red Triangles, Gays and Lesbian with Pink Squares, the Roma and in 1941, and an attempt to eradicate European Jewry with a mocking gold Star of David sown into the anonymous black and white striped uniforms worn by all of those women and men, girls and boys transported around Europe to the industrial death camps. No, never reduce humans to cattle because you play with fire, that very elemental spark which makes us human. You can ascertain why the maxim of Socrates may not have been particularly welcomed in the Cave. After all we were little more than cattle in Plato's thought experiment, In fact his whole schema as delineated in *The Republic* placed the workers at the bottom, the military just above and those in flowing robes of white who were the philosophers at the pinnacle. The latter was very convenient and congenial for them.

Why was I with men considered to resemble the bovine. It is rather straightforward because I too had been a pupil off a philosopher. I had attempted a little Socratic Discourse, but it was not approved off. A little too clever for my own good was the unspoken reaction. Don't let the pupil get any grandiose pretensions they sniggered. Although I pursued my course of asking rhetorical questions.
Plato had said:
'Hemlock or you can help me in a little philosophising. I want to prove the validity of my ideas about universals, Forms, and you are just the kind of material I am looking for, a sort of participation philosopher on the spot. What do you say?'
The bizarre thing is that it was presented as a choice, free will.

I replied:
'I was always interested in the practical application of philosophy, …your philosophy, Master.'
'Good, that is settled then. The Elite Guard will escort you to the grand enterprise,'
He nodded to a few rather robust soldiers and that was how it had all begun.

4.

But no, the animal fat was not to ease the open wounds which were encrusted with congealed blood caused by the now rusted shackles but to thicken the warden's gruel. This was like the moment a child realises the world is not a pleasant place and then I was confronted with the enigma. Was I to attempt to escape this imprisonment only to see the shadows were indeed caused by the fire or to foster discontent amongst the slaves in the cave? For I had already seen the other side of the fire, what lay beyond the Cave's gapping mouth and had nearly had to drink hemlock as my punishment for questioning the master philosophers. *Should I* attempt to negotiate some kind of truce between the elite philosophers and myself or did the resolution to this puzzle somehow lie in these men treated as cattle. The solution erupted into my head with the intensity of pure amphetamine taken intravenously. My mind was cold clear and crystal. The resolution lay in the slaves and soldiers realising their common social class which was not of the philosophers. A text written centuries later tumbled into my mind. George Orwell '*1984*', and the quotation from that misappropriated text that was strung across my lighting zig-zag consciousness was: 'If there is hope it lies with the proles.' But the proletariat were self-evidently only interested in whether their gruel was thick or thin or those in the cave. The soldiers although only marginally better off wallowed in the etch on the ruler of power and status and the philosophers had the banter to convince all was well in Athens. But different days would come Spartacus would rise and rise again resplendent. That could never, ever be quenched.

5.

I removed an eminently well concealed package of hemlock from under my testicles and slipped it into a particularly unappetising bowl of insipid gruel. There was no alternative in these circumstances but 'the living flame' will always contest the darkest night of History because 'the darker the night the brighter the star. 'My name, Walter, Walter Benjamin

Ward 20, a boy amongst men and Paraldehyde.
(a story told from multiple points of view.)

Ernie, who was pleased to see me back on the light gang, pressed another yellow capsule into my hand. His face looked puckered like Charles Bukowski's, but Ernie was no poet. The capsule was a barbiturate called Nembutal; it would both wobble your mind but gave you a hazy buzz as well. Ernie, a man in his fifties had been prescribed these little beauties by ignorant quacks since his marriage. He had also been attending the hospital as a day patient to work on the garden's weekdays since that moment of matrimonial bliss which was immediately previous to the birth of a child. He never mentioned the child, only it's conception. I wanted to be 'clean' and had thought it would be safe now I was in a hospital. That was an illusion as you will discover.

'Thanks, Ernie I will drop it later.'

'There are more where that came from'. He smiled with the barbiturate saliva encrusted around his mouth.

I mooched between the potting sheds and the Adolescent Unit until the coaches taking the day-patients, lurched away. There was a drain in near the Unit where I would unobtrusively drop these yellow submarines. However, Nembutal would be only one of my challenges and worries.

'Hello Noel.'

'Sister Leonard I was just on my way back to the Unit.'

'You had better hurry up or Auntie Edith will be chasing me out of a job and you back to 20's.' She said while simultaneously smiling.

Auntie Edith was my name for the consultant, a true bluestocking. There was not much that Sister Leonard did not know about nursing under sixteens, apparently. For reasons that seemed unfathomable she had married a reptile of a man. The deputy-head gardener, John. He would evoke a combination of anger and embarrassment while he would tell intimate stories about himself and Sister Leonard in the potting shed. However, his repertoire was very limited.

The urn chugged away on the hissing gas ring. Nine thirty and Fred as I am known, the gardener's assistant, had thrown in the tea, milk and sugar. It would be sure to be ready at eleven sharp and there were the cheese sandwiches to make yet. The heavy and light gangs were at work on the gardens. Victor, the head gardener was making cuttings in the glass house for the flowers which embellished some, well most, of the wards. The asylum I work in was like a clock whose cogs turned perfectly. That if they were wound correctly and not dropped down a drain. There was an excellent drainage system in this place. I have heard it called part monastery, part prison dependent on the state of mind of the voices. It was generally presumed by those living outside that it was an asylum. No, it was a psychiatric hospital. There are medicines handed out, syrups given, injections hammered home and electric shocks, not for those under fifteen though. But the rest, well yes. Let us not make bones about their ages? After all we would all be dust someday or so many have claimed I had heard somewhere.

Sister Leonard mused as she measured out the tots of brown syrup Chlorpromazine, for her patients on the Adolescent Unit what a fine man her husband John and how wonderful that secret night of passion on a Cornish Beach had been. Something that she and her soul partner would reminisce in quiet moments about all their lives. Whoops, mustn't be giving the kids too much Largactil as she gathered her thoughts. That was the medicine ready for lunch. Efficiency is the sign of a good ward sister she smiled. Again her thoughts wandered; such a shame about Noel, he was a nice lad but had got mixed up with the wrong crowd. The very words her mother had attempted to expunge her love of John with, parents!!

Joan was a handful, that is certainly correct I pondered. I shall bring disarray and chaos to this Unit. They say I am not ill. That stupid doctor had called me 'a spoilt little rich girl.' I don't understand why Noel will not be my boyfriend? I have done acid, speed, the lot. Could show him a better time than any of these nymphets on this Unit, what is it I puzzled. I will smuggle in some acid, that will do the trick. I will buy it on weekend leave. Why don't all the kids get weekend leave and why do a few, including Noel, get transferred to adult wards. Nobody transfers me anywhere except Mother and Father to this god forsaken place. 'To give you a little time to think about your behaviour.' At least I have some "behaviour ". There lives are so damned boring: no drugs, no kinks of any kind as far as I can gather.

Yes, the Lysergic Acid arrived and no one wanted to take it. Least of all me. She was not a nice person but stood a chance once she'd driven everyone else to distraction. That was why I did not sleep with her. She was a beauty but sometimes there is just a wrong thing to do. Indeed six months later on one of my early day passes to buy books at Hudson's in the city centre spotted me wearing a posh school uniform and cid create a leather briefcase. She glanced up, I looked away. It was for the best. The acid created mayhem but no one was caught. Perhaps the nursing staff turned a blind eye...

Dear Auntie had sent me down to Ward 20 again. An adult but open ward. It was single sex like all the wards except for the Unit and Lambo Ward, mixed non-acute adult admission. Wards 19 & 5 being locked male and woman's admission wards, while 20s and 10s were the same accept but unlocked. I had got to know the staff quite well. Some would me books and we would debate matters philosophical, theological, psychological and literary. It was at this hospital that I was introduced to the ideas of Carl Jung and his Noble Prize Winner writer friend Herman Hesse. These later ideas were developed by a memorable senior registrar on the Unit, Helen.

However, I am on my timed return visits both to the Unit and the Gardens when a very poorly man in his forties is brought in convinced he was a cook-coo. He is a lecturer from Birmingham University but has lost the plot to the extent that play was over. The staff ask me to find if he had taken Lysergic Acid, he had. I had never seen anything akin to this. He could se his feathers and kept jumping off tables, beds, wardrobes, anything and waving his arms. They interview injected him with Chlorpromazine, Haloperidol but nothing brought him down. Ward 20 was a bungalow and he tried to get onto the roof. This is three days and nights later, L.S.D. wears off after about eight hours. The door was so well unhinged no one could close it. The consultant arrives and leaves and the charge-nurse begins to draw up another injection into a glass syringe.

'What are you giving him now. Why the glass syringe.' I ask.

'Noel, this would melt any plastic one.'
'What is it called.'

'Paraldehyde.

Easter and beyond.

And what excess of love bewildered them till they died?
I write it out in verse MacDonald and MacBride
And Connelly and Pearse
Now and in time to be, Whenever green is worn,
Are changed, changed utterly
A terrible beauty is born
- W. B. Yeats *Easter 1916*. [extract] (1988) pp 296-298.

You may wonder what I was doing in Finsbury Park. We Catholics are indeed everywhere we are ubiquitous. Here in England many think of us as almost like dirty pests. Although we had always observed their behaviour with interest and often alarm. We always travelled light and took notes on those who regarded us as parasites. This is my tale, the tale of an everyday Mary. A woman who had a variety of Holy statues in her flat: The Sacred Heart of Jesus, Our Lady Immaculate and lived with her teenage son. I am a trinity: a single mother, my son and that echo in my mind which is my father who had seen the inside of the H-Blocks.

A gust of cold wind whirled into my small council flat in North London and I shivered as I saw a faint spectral almost undefinable figure hover briefly above my Holy statues. These broken windows were becoming a problem; the neighbours were gossiping; the social worker was becoming suspicious and simply the price of paying the glazier was becoming a task in itself. I had many tribulations and the consensus woven into the local fabric was that they mainly emanated from Joseph, my son. People said it was a little more than the usual growing pains all teenagers are stung with when they stumble into that hornet's

nest of metamorphosis called adolescence. I swept up the slivers of glass and called a glazier who I did business with yet again. There was no question of a call to the council for repairs as they had begun asking awkward questions. He replaced the window, puttied it in and said:
'I hope you don't mind me saying this, but it is costing you a fortune Mary. You must be pleased I did the job on the cheap.'
I tried not to grimace lowering a veil of lace and then replied:
'And I hope you would not be concerned if I said that it helps keep you in business, Mr O'Connor. The reasons I ring you are purely one's of business not social work, you understand.'
'Alright, alright. I was only trying to help.'
He huffed and puffed out and slammed the front door. I noted a swagger in his walk. Maybe he thought himself better or was he afraid of the supposedly unpredictable behaviour of those who lived in our area. Or he could be undercover?
Fidgeting more than usual when my eyes noticed what the time was. I wondered where my son had got to and then as if by synchronicity he erupted into the room:
'Where have you been?'
'Hi yeah mum, I was only at the Mosque.'
'Now what is a Catholic boy doing in a Mosque? That is not to say I am against interfaith relations. That one has got a bit of a reputation now in Finsbury Park and with the Brits generally. I have heard they have been some quite extreme preachers there:
'They are not called preachers, but Imams. Mother.'

'Alright but be careful Joe. I don't want a convert on my hands as that would take some explaining.' We smiled at each other in a pact of reassurance; pacts lead to the signing of Treaties and we both knew a Treaty is not worth the paper or ink.

I had been going to Mass on a more regular footing since the windows had been smashed and replaced so many times. What I could not ascertain was why they were being bricked. Some local people knew my father had been in "the 'army', the 'Provo's'" during the war in the North and had done time in 'The Maze'. That was why I had left, well sort of anyway. There is a grapevine you would only understand if you came from a Republican family. It spreads in two ways, both in the community and to the Brits. I knew it had been a mistake to attend that meeting to set up a steering committee for an event to mark the centenary. One hundred years since Easter 1916 and the blood sacrifice of Connolly, Pearse, MacBride and others. I had been taught to recite Padraig Pearse's last words at his execution before I could read and became lost in clouds condensed from memory and reverie which then rained words:

"The fools, the fools! - They have left us our Fenian dead, and while Ireland holds these graves, Ireland unfree shall never be at peace."

I had not noticed that Joe had buzzed backed into the front room where I had remained after he stomped off to his bedroom:

'Stop it, stop that bloody crap mum. We both know that you were tarred -and-feathered when you got pregnant the first time. Whatever happened to the child mother? Was it a boy or a girl? Eh!' Joseph screamed and sobbed almost simultaneously.

'Mary, Mother of God, I swear those words just came out Joseph.'

I said this in a measured voice which was a method learnt as a child. Joe had become just like my father in some ways, but he had no cause and would not have had the discipline to fight for one if he did, I guessed, I believed. Easter came and went with a slightly increased dissident Republican activity in the North, but nothing that my father would have considered sufficient to rouse sleeping Eire. I now know for certain the War was over. If the dissidents couldn't orchestrate a couple of spectaculars and the masses was quiescence on the centenary of the blood sacrifice of Easter 1916. It really was finished. The truth slapped me in the face as brutally as any R.U.C officer had done to generations of Catholic women. Maybe it was just as well Sinn Féin had adopted a Pan-Nationalist electoral policy which may create a United Ireland eventually, an Irish Workers Socialist Republic I now very much doubted. That apparition appeared before me a second time. This time it was possible to perceive some of its features. It was a shimmer that was both pale and emaciated with long dark hair. I kept these matters to myself because I had an aunt who was detained in Manchester under the Mental Health Act on Section 2 and was in the language of her doctors:

Migrated to Section 3 so we can make sure she has

the full range of therapeutic interventions for her benefit.

Another letter had said she was forced to have medication and that made me shudder more than any ghost could have done. Joe had departed from the house and a silence as dense as crystal filled the void. I repressed thoughts of his father. Though I was becoming concerned about Joseph's increasing interest in a politicized version of a very fundamentalist Islam. It was beginning to dominate him. I was opposed to this on two levels. Firstly, there was the question of Roman Catholicism and secondly, that of the potential for violence and wrongheaded violence at that. It seemed my father's activity had been justified. But to get involved with a group who may well have been originally a Frankenstein created by the West. It was heresy politically and they were really an apocalyptic cult. This was a qualitatively different situation to what had existed in Ireland and I had to draw a line. The line was soon crossed! The police arrived, they knew me or at least of me and my background. Joe had been arrested and was being questioned about 'conspiring with others to prepare for an act of terrorism.' Although as the conversation developed, I ascertained he hadn't as yet been charged.

'Hail Mary, full of grace, pray for us sinners, now and at the hour of our death'. I said with a stony silence.

It had become a pre-recorded response of Irish Catholics in these situations. A forty-eight-hour order was extended by the Home Sectary to twenty-eight days. No one in the official or unofficial Republican movement would sully their hands with this one. I was told in the deep recesses of an anonymous pub:

'It would not be in the wider interests of building momentum in the rank and file towards an end game of Irish Emancipation.'

'So, my son who is the teenage grandchild of a man who had been subjected to the horrors of the H-Blocks was now expendable because he had an inconvenient ideology'

'There would be no legal assistance. The decision has been made by the Army Council who as you have always known Mary is the legitimate government of Ireland being the direct inheritors of the authority of Dáil Eiermann.'

'A question of bloody 'Ecco Homo'1 more like.'

In the Vulgate Bible the Latin phrase: 'Ecco Homo' or 'Behold the human' is said by Pontius Pilate as he washes his hands in an attempt to free himself of guilt for the crucifixion of Jesus of Nazareth.

It was a dark, very bleak and wet journey back to Finsbury Park. When I reached home, I arrived drenched by the cold rain and threw myself onto my bed without changing my sodden clothes.

Whether I developed a fever I shall never know. A third apparition came towards me. This time there was no mistaking the figure, it was Bobby Sands, the first hunger striker to die in 1981 a poet and an elected M.P. His life and poetry were familiar to me; he had the status of a secular saint in Republican circles and beyond. He said tenderly:

'Mary, do you understand now W. B. Yeats was correct when he wrote in his poem *Easter 1916*: "Too long a sacrifice/Can make a stone of the heart"

I awoke in a fever and my clothes were soaked with sweat and I knew my life had been irrevocably changed. Fortunately, Joe was released without charge as the evidence would not have stood in court. It was flimsy and circumstantial. A few weeks later in the afternoon we received a surprise visit from Mr. O'Connor. To his astonishment I immediately welcomed him into our little concrete nest. He sat down and without hesitation begun:

'This may come as a quite a shock to you. I am your uncle, your father's brother. He was killed on 'active service' and that is all you need to know. It is the Veterans branch of Sinn Fenn that now preserves Ireland's cultural heritage since the Good Friday Agreement, you understand?'

'Yes, yes of course.'

'They have bought you, Joe and someone Joe has never met. A young woman you last saw as a new-born.'

Joe exclaimed:

'There was no abortion?!'

O'Connor continued:

'They have bought a cottage in the rural West for the three of you. You will never 'want for anything."

'Joe, it looks like you have a family after all.' I said.

'And perhaps we all have a future.' He replied

Our 'future' in Ireland was almost an idyll until the banking crash and recession of 2008. But although our endowments and thus, our income dropped life was warm in our cottage. A warmth of family and of gradually being accepted into the far spread but close-knit local community. How different from our lives in Finsbury Park, I thought. But prosperity brings many blessings but poverty or at least a lack of a surplus bring other spirits calling. Joe had inherited the spirits of revolt and it was enflamed by when he began to read about the social problems we were having in the Republic, the lack of housing while millionaires dined on Venison ,the water-rates had become a big issue as well and the continuing question of partition were often on his lips. They were not merely the concerns of the young though. with the Unionist vote now a minority in the North it began to look like a 'revolution in a ballot box' was a real possibility. Sinn Fenn had done remarkably well in the election in the South, together with some far-Left groups. There was talk of a minority progressive Left government in the Dáil.

Yet there was something else very profound that nagged at Joe. To be sure it was rebel blood. I knew it and as he grew-up so did he. Rebellion was in our blood. Not something to be treated with leeches or sedatives. My country was built on the tombs of Republicans and socialists like James Connolly. Because ours was a land not only of bogs and mists, it was fertile with the blood of the men and women who had created it, died for it and been murdered for their courage. The Eucharistic sacrifice. Joe was now a young man, no longer a teenager, and I had taken to wearing shawls and headscarves. I knitted thick (mock) Gaelic jumpers for sale to gullible tourists, mostly Americans but also a growing number of Brits. When would Joe find a girl, I wondered in my heart? Or a male partner for ours is a country transformed after the disgrace of the Church. Ireland had chosen an openly Gay Taoiseach in 2017, but he was no revolutionary, let me be clear. However, Sinn Fenn argued for Gay and Lesbian Rights in this humming new Ireland.

Still, my heart and head were bothered. Joe had been away at a Gaelic Football competition with some of the local young men. The knock on the door which every Irish woman of my generation fears came about 1.00 a.m. However, they spoke not with British accents but were Garda officers both uniformed and plain-clothes. Joe had been caught running arms to the North for the Continuity or as it is known the Real I.R.A. I knew it was the truth this time.

Joe was just like my father and had rebel blood coursing through his veins. I wept, I know not why as I mused, maybe he was the incarnation of the 'model' Irish child that was never conceived by W. B. Yeats and Maud Gonne. If you came from my land and background your heart would also almost burst with pride. That is something you will never understand unless you had come from an oppressed people. So, I prepared for the years of prison visits that lay ahead, or maybe not I smiled inwardly?

Petra, daughter of the revolution and her life after release from Stammheim Prison (A tale about the S.P.K).

The dark allurement of revolution and sweet aroma of
introspection are intertwining like phantoms in this squat in
1975. Petra, a small round woman of 19 is sitting in the
smog of contemplation. Her hair is brown, untidy and short, it
sits on her head like the crown of a recently resurrected
Rosa Luxemburg. A brown tee-shirt with embroidered
flowers around the neck emphases her plump physic and
faded tight black jeans combine to say that she is a goddess
of the underground and nymph of primordial night. Smiling
vaguely at a middle-aged man who looks like he comes out
of some 19th century Russian novel, perhaps he keeps a
chronicle of the demise of his shrink into madness, she
suppresses a smile:

'Comrade…but let's just cut the shit baby, what kind of crap
are you lying down'.
Peter slowly strokes a long ginger beard which seems
temporarily, to Petra, to be creeping across the roach littered
floorboards like a startled lizard.
 He mumbles: 'It's like the movement needs a push to tip the
balance, the proletariat are in the mood for poetry, we have
to become their calligraphers, you dig'.
She sighs: 'O I dig man, I really dig, know what I mean'
 The rapid rattle of a typewriter sends waves of disturbance
through their awareness, it's like an automatic rifle firing into
a black chasm of zero, like the relentless march of the
masses into nirvana, muses Petra. In her mind there are
images like water forming into vapour, into clouds which
sometimes obscure the sun, now they spill their seed upon
soil in a shower or in a deluge, either to fertilize seed or to
wash it away in a torrent. Peter is pondering whether he
should scatter a little fertilizer in this garden, the Garden of
Love, where iconoclasts are welcome and encouraged to
participate in its rites. But he decides, with a jolt from the
intellect, that everything is subordinated to the struggle. He
wonders what the dynamic of the armed struggle is, some of
its shadows were illuminated and a solution had surfaced
during those group therapy sessions with the professor, now
imprisoned himself for activities against the State and

Capital, where they had discussed the dialectics of liberation. They had discovered that for them, those especially damaged by capitalism, that their situation was more complex than for their comrades without psychiatric problems, their liberation from illness was directly linked to active participation in the emancipation of all the oppressed, it must be an attempt to grasp the full implications of the "death of God", but more than that, it was to be an active assassination of God, of the patriarch and of all his oppressive relationships and the, consequent, rebirth of the child.

He murmurs to Petra:

'The struggle, all of it, is about regaining innocence lost when we were children.'

A shadow passes across Petra's face: 'Yea man, you're talking 'bout the armed struggle, call it just cool baby, self-realization, just getting rid of all the shit they put in the head.'

Peter says: '"Have you read the poetry of Sylvia Plath?'

'Of course, 'Daddy'…that's hot poetry, it's really groovy."

'Sylvia had grasped something of the essence when she wrote that line: "Daddy I had to kill you"'.

Petra becomes animated; a crimson flush was rising in her face:

'She wrote those lines, there're like furrows in my mind, yea know, "Daddy, daddy, you bastard, I'm through" that's just real man, wow, so real. I've something to tell you, I'm Lady Lazarus, yea know, like in the poem'.

Peter's gaze tightens; he looks intently at this young woman:

'You attempted suicide?'

'Yea, I guess I did'.

'Do you have a name comrade?' 'They call me Petra.'

The incessant bashing on the typewriter continues without relief, it is thumping through the wall and invading Petra and Peter's consciousness. This is the remorseless beating of History:

'I have a name, it is Peter. Take my hand daughter, daughter of the revolution'

A loud explosion, a blaze of orange light flashes into the room, black smoke billows and then their disembodied screams re reverberate in the chaos:

'Shit, man this is heavy!!'

Hard and sharpened steel voices jab them like poisoned
spear heads:
'Freeze it's the police… don't move, down, get down you
scum'
 Petra and Peter are thrown against the floor, then heaved
up and pinned to the wall:
Peter shouts: 'Resist them.'
Petra yells: 'Defy them baby, I love you.'

But Peter loved only one thing and that was the 'armed
struggle.' He clenched his teeth until a carefully, indeed,
medically concealed, cyanide capsule ruptured. Petra was
stripped naked on the floor of a West German police wagon.,
sirens wailing, red lights flashing with a plastic gag rammed
securely into her mouth but although Petra looked Eastward
and had believed what Ulrike Meinhoff had said about
'actual existing socialism' in the East.' She had not been fully
trained, either behind the Iron Curtain or the Middle East.
   Like the majority of the Red Army Faction/ Socialist
Patients Collective members who did not die during
commando activities or meet in a similar fate in Stammheim
Prison they threw the book at Petra. Decades in the
purpose-built prison until release as a State Pardon. As
Astrid Proll, a comrade, has said: 'What exactly do they
expect them to do?'
      Petra threw herself into work helping refugees in
Germany, now Unified. But as W. B. Yeats noted 'too long a
struggle makes a heart of stone.' Petra was 'star crossed',
she did not stand a chance. She used a new generation of
contacts and blew herself up outside a police station.
Although, you may not be surprised that she left a document
explaining that this was her nemesis for Peter's death. Petra
never knew nor was told about the cyanide capsule that he
haemorrhaged to take his own life. As D.H. Lawrence said:
'never trust the artist, trust the tale.'

Lightning Source UK Ltd.
Milton Keynes UK
UKHW022044050321
379874UK00016B/1265/J

9 781783 825233